THE BATTLE OF CHANCELLORSVILLE
CIVIL WAR SERIES

TEXT BY GARY W. GALLAGHER

Maps by George Skoch

Thanks to Robert Krick and Donald Pfanz at Fredericksburg and Spotsylvania National Military Park.

Published by Eastern National Park and Monument Association, copyright 1995.

Eastern National Park & Monument Association aids and promotes the historical, scientific and educational activities of the National Park Service. It also supports research, interpretation and conservation programs of the Service. As a nonprofit cooperating association recognized by Congress, it makes interpretive material available to park visitors and the general public.

Cover: *Eve of the Storm,* by Don Troiani, courtesy of Historical Art Prints, Ltd., Southbury, Connecticut.

Back cover: *Last Meeting of Lee and Jackson,* by Everett B. D. Julio, courtesy of The Museum of the Confederacy, Richmond, Virginia.

Printed on recycled paper.

THE BATTLE OF CHANCELLORSVILLE

*M*ay 1863 opened in a burst of spring glory along the Rappahannock River. Blossoms from apple, peach, and cherry trees splashed color against a background of soft green woods. Wildflowers dotted hillsides and ditches alongside rolling fields of luxuriant grasses and wheat half a foot high. Nature thus masked the scars inflicted by two huge armies over the previous months, providing a beautiful stage across which a whirlwind of action would be played out during May's first week. Armed with an excellent strategic blueprint, Union Major General Joseph Hooker and his Army of the Potomac marched into this scene of pastoral renewal. General Robert E. Lee and Lieutenant General Thomas J. "Stonewall" Jackson

reacted with a series of maneuvers that carried their fabled collaboration to its dazzling apogee. The confrontation produced a grand drama filled with memorable scenes, a vivid contrast in personalities between the respective army commanders, and dogged fighting by soldiers on both sides. Its final act brought humiliating defeat for the proud Army of the Potomac and problematical victory for the Army of Northern Virginia.

The spring of 1863 marked the advent of the third year in an increasingly bloody war. Along the Mississippi River, Major General Ulysses S. Grant continued his movement against the Confederate stronghold at Vicksburg with an eye toward establishing Union control of the "Father of Waters." In Middle Tennessee, Major General William S. Rosecrans and the Army of the Cumberland prepared to engage General Braxton Bragg's Confederate Army of Tennessee in operations that could settle the fate of Chattanooga and the Georgia hinterlands. The last major military arena lay in Virginia, where the armies of Hooker and Lee were arrayed along the Rappahannock River.

Neither government considered Virginia the most important theater. President Abraham Lincoln and Major General Henry W. Halleck, his general in chief, considered Grant's operations most important. Success there would separate the Trans-Mississippi states from the rest of the Confederacy, allow Northern vessels to cruise the river at will, and provide waterborne access to great stretches of Confederate territory. Lincoln and Halleck saw Rosecrans's movements as second in importance, judging Hooker's activities a clear third. On the Confederate side, Jefferson Davis and many of his generals believed the decisive fighting would come in Tennessee. A group that has come to be known as the "Western Concentration Bloc," which included officers such as General Joseph E. Johnston and Lieutenant General James Longstreet as well as

Senator Louis T. Wigfall of Texas and other influential politicians, argued that Lee's army should be weakened to reinforce Braxton Bragg's Army of Tennessee. Lee thought otherwise and hoped to keep as much strength as possible under his command. Mulling over the strategic situation in late February, he had postulated victory for the Confederacy through "systematic success" on the battlefield that would create "a revolution among [the Northern] people."

Lee knew better than most that military success in Virginia stood the best chance of triggering such a revolution. Accused then and later of wearing Virginia blinders, the Southern commander in fact understood that the psychological power of his victories probably outweighed whatever the Confederacy might accomplish elsewhere. The eastern theater contained the respective capitals, each nation's largest army, and the Confederacy's most famous generals, Lee and Jackson. The Mississippi River or Middle Tennessee might be more crucial in a strictly military sense, but many citizens and politicians North and South, as well as virtually all foreign observers, considered the eastern theater to be transcendent. Lincoln had learned this lesson the previous year, when a series of Union victories in the West had been overshadowed by Major General George B. McClellan's failure during the Seven Days' battles. "It seems unreasonable," the frustrated president had observed, "that a series of successes, extending through

half-a-year, and clearing more than a hundred thousand square miles of country, should help us so little, while a single half-defeat should hurt us so much." The campaign between Hooker and Lee—the one man new to army leadership and the other a consummate field commander—would have great significance because so many people considered it the war's centerpiece in the spring of 1863.

The rival commanders and their armies offered a study in contrasts on the eve of the campaign. Hooker had been named to head the Army of the Potomac on January 25, 1863, through a combination of solid service and effective political maneuvering. A graduate of West Point, who ranked twenty-ninth in the class of 1837, he had left the army in the 1850s but accepted a brigadier generalcy of volunteers shortly after war erupted in 1861. He

AS THE CAMPAIGN OPENED, JOE HOOKER BRIMMED WITH SELF-CONFIDENCE. "MY PLANS ARE PERFECT," HE TOLD A GROUP OF OFFICERS, "AND WHEN I START TO CARRY THEM OUT, MAY GOD HAVE MERCY ON GENERAL LEE, FOR I WILL HAVE NONE."

(LC)

CHANCELLORSVILLE WAS A LARGE BRICK HOUSE IN THE WILDERNESS, RATHER THAN A TOWN AS ITS NAME MIGHT IMPLY. ORIGINALLY OPERATED AS A TAVERN, IT BECAME HOOKER'S HEADQUARTERS DURING THE BATTLE.

(BL)

missed the battle of First Bull Run, then fought as a division and corps chief at the Seven Days, Second Bull Run, Antietam, and Fredericksburg. A press report of action on the Peninsula headed "Fighting— Joe Hooker" had been rendered "Fighting Joe Hooker" when it appeared in print, thus fastening on its subject a nickname that he despised but never managed to shake. Still, he did stand out as an aggressive officer in an army blessed with too little of that commodity. A shameless self-promoter, Hooker worked tirelessly to supplant Major General Ambrose E. Burnside following the Union fiasco at Fredericksburg and the equally ignominious Mud March of mid-January 1863. Telling Republicans in Congress what they wanted to hear, touting his own accomplishments, and criticizing Burnside, he emerged in late January as the president's choice to lead the Army of the Potomac.

Hooker looked the part of a general and exuded self-assurance. Above medium height, blue-eyed, with light hair and a ruddy complexion, he cut a dashing figure on or off a horse. "It is no vanity in me to say I am a damned sight better general than any you had on that field," he had told Lincoln after First Bull Run. Newspapers generally liked Hooker's cockiness. One rhapsodized about him in January 1863 as "a General of the heroic stamp. . . . who

feels the enthusiasm of a soldier and who loves battle from an innate instinct for his business."

The president told his new commander what he expected in a remarkably perceptive and blunt letter. "I believe you to be a brave and skillful soldier . . . ," wrote Lincoln. "You have confidence in yourself, which is a valuable, if not an indispensable quality. You are ambitious, which, within reasonable bounds, does good rather than harm." But Lincoln knew Hooker had worked against Burnside—which "did a great wrong to the country"—and had spoken of the need for a military dictator if the North were to win the war. "Of course it was not for this, but in spite of it, that I have given you the command," continued the president: "Only those generals who gain successes, can set up dictators. What I now ask of you is military success, and I will risk the dictatorship."

In a communication dated January 31, 1863, Halleck spoke for Lincoln in reiterating to Hooker what he had told Burnside earlier that month: "Our first object was, not Richmond, but the defeat and scattering of Lee's army." The president confirmed Halleck's language some two months later, observing that "our prime object is the enemies' army in front of us, and is not with, or about, Richmond."

The Army of the Potomac in January 1863 represented a poor weapon with which Hooker might smite the Rebels. "Fighting Joe" inherited an organization

LINCOLN'S LETTER TO HOOKER

Executive Mansion,
Washington, January 26, 1863

Major General Hooker:

General,

I have placed you at the head of the Army of the Potomac. Of course I have done this upon what appears to me to be sufficient reasons, and yet I think it best for you to know that there are some things in regard to which I am not quite satisfied with you. I believe you to be a brave and skillful soldier, which, of course, I like. I also believe you do not mix politics with your profession, in which you are right. You have confidence in yourself, which is a valuable if not indispensable, quality.

You are ambitious, which, within reasonable bounds, does good rather than harm; but I think that during General Burnside's command of the army you have taken counsel of your ambition, and thwarted him as much as you could, in which you did a great wrong to the country and to a most meritorious and honorable brother officer. I have heard, in such way as to believe it, of your recently saying that both the Army and the Government needed a Dictator. Of course it was not for this, but in spite of it, that I have given you the command. Only those generals who gain successes can set up dictators. What I now ask of you is military success, and I will risk the dictatorship. The Government will support you

to the utmost of its ability, which is neither more nor less than it has done and will do for all commanders. I much fear that the spirit which you have aided to infuse into the army, of criticising their commander and withholding confidence from him, will now turn upon you. I shall assist you as far as I can to put it down. Neither you nor Napoleon, if he were alive again, could get any good out of an army while such a spirit prevails in it. And now beware of rashness. Beware of rashness, but with energy and sleepless vigilance go forward, and give us victories.

Yours very truly,
A. Lincoln

> *"Only those generals who gain successes, can set up dictators. What I now ask of you is military success, and I will risk the dictatorship."*

---

buffeted by defeat, lacking confidence in leaders who engaged in bitter squabbling, plagued by breakdowns in the delivery of pay and food, and suffering a high rate of desertion. An officer in the 140th New York described an "entire army struck with melancholy. . . . The mind of the army, just now, is a sort of intellectual marsh in which False Report grows fat, and sweeps up and down with a perfect audacity and fierceness." Another soldier thought "the army is fast approaching a mob." A man in the 155th Pennsylvania spoke darkly of the dismantling of Hooker's force: "I like the idea for my part," he observed, "& I think they may as well abandon this part of Virginia's bloody soil." Many of the problems boiled down to the men's lack of faith in their generals. "From want of confidence in its leaders and from no other reason," summarized one observant New Yorker, "the army is fearfully demoralized."

Hooker took a number of steps that quickly restored morale. He named as medical director Jonathan Letterman, who

oversaw improvements in food and sanitation that helped to lower the incidence of illness among the soldiers. Tackling the problem of desertion, Hooker tightened patrols while also convincing Lincoln to issue a proclamation of amnesty. A new system of furloughs for individuals and units with strong records went into effect, a measure, noted one man, that triggered "joyous anticipation" in the ranks. Known as a general who appreciated good drink, Hooker mandated a whiskey ration for sol-

MORALE IN THE ARMY OF THE POTOMAC WAS AT LOW EBB AT THE TIME HOOKER ASSUMED COMMAND. HE WOULD HAVE JUST THREE MONTHS TO TURN THINGS AROUND.

(BL)

CORPS BADGES OF THE ARMY OF THE POTOMAC UNDER HOOKER.

FIRST
SECOND
FIFTH
THIRD
CAVALRY
SIXTH
NINTH
ELEVENTH
TWELFTH

artillery because soldiers "regarded their batteries with a feeling of devotion." But its principal effect was to deny Northern artillery the ability to mass for concentrated fire. Hooker took the opposite approach with his mounted arm, which he gathered into a Cavalry Corps under the direction of Major General George Stoneman.

diers returning from picket duty. Perhaps most important symbolically, the new commander instituted a system of corps badges. Initially aimed at identifying the units of shirkers, the badges soon became highly valued symbols that engendered pride in belonging to a particular corps. Hooker probably did not exaggerate when he commented after the war that this innovation "had a magical effect on the discipline and conduct of our troops. . . . The badge became very precious in the estimation of the soldier."

The army also underwent reorganization. Hooker scrapped the Grand Divisions of Burnside's tenure, which had grouped the Union corps into larger administrative bodies. This required that he communicate with eight corps—a cumbersome arrangement at best. Major General Oliver Otis Howard, who led the Eleventh Corps, suggested that Hooker opted for this arrangement because he "enjoyed maneuvering several independent bodies." Far more pernicious was Hooker's decision to scatter the army's artillery batteries among its infantry divisions, which removed the able Brigadier General Henry J. Hunt from effective charge of the Federal long arm. Hooker believed this move would promote strong bonds between the infantry and

A canvass of Hooker's subordinate command reveals some competence and a good deal of caution, but no brilliance. Closest to Hooker was Third Corps commander Daniel E. Sickles, a former New York congressman who had murdered his wife's lover in 1859, won acquittal, and then—to the astonishment of Washington

GEORGE STONEMAN COMMANDED THE UNION ARMY'S CAVALRY CORPS. "LET YOUR WATCHWORD BE FIGHT," HOOKER TOLD HIM.

(BL)

society—accepted Mrs. Sickles back into his home. Innocent of military training and beholden to Hooker for his advancement to major general, Sickles differed from the other corps chiefs in his aggressiveness on the battlefield. The First Corps belonged to Major General John F. Reynolds, a handsome Pennsylvanian widely known then and since as the ablest corps commander in the army—but whose record offers little evidence to substantiate that lofty reputation. Major General Darius N. Couch, a Pennsylvanian who led the Second Corps, emulated his idol George B. McClellan with a conservative approach to war and politics. A third Pennsylvanian, Major General George G. Meade, quietly presided over the Fifth Corps after a solid but unspectacular record during the first two years of the conflict. A pair of strong McClellan supporters, Major General John Sedgwick and Major General Henry W. Slocum, commanded the Sixth and Twelfth corps respectively. Neither had compiled a distinguished record; indeed, Sedgwick's one memorable episode as a general consisted of leading his division to ignominious disaster in the West Woods at Antietam. Except for Sickles, all of these men had advanced partly because of their ability to mask conservative political views in the context of a war shifting to a more radical orientation concerning emancipation and other issues.

O. O. Howard of the Eleventh Corps stood out as a pious Republican among predominantly Democratic peers. Hooker shared Howard's politics but not his moral code. In a postwar interview, the former army commander remarked savagely that Howard "was always a woman among troops. . . . If he was not born in petticoats, he ought to have been, and ought to wear them. He was always taken up with Sunday Schools and the temperance cause." Howard inspired little devotion in his corps, which counted among its ranks thousands of Germans who would have preferred Major General Carl Schurz or some other German-speaking officer as their commander. Taunted as "Dutchmen" throughout the army, the soldiers of the Eleventh Corps stood apart from their comrades— just as their commander stood apart from them. Adversity would bind them together in the wake of Chancellorsville.

Despite the uncertain quality of many of its senior generals, the Army of the Potomac approached the spring campaign as a formidable force. Well supplied and equipped and vigorously led by Hooker, the army numbered nearly 134,000 men of all arms and could carry 413 artillery pieces into battle. Hooker described this host as "the finest army on the planet." Others shared this view, including Edward Porter Alexander, a perceptive Confederate artillerist who after the war wrote of "Hooker's great army—the greatest this country had ever seen."

A series of reviews through the spring season allowed the army to display its growing confidence and power. President Lincoln joined Hooker in early April to preside over the most notable of these public showings. Scores of thousands of men marched by the admiring general and their commander in chief. After one of

GEORGE G. MEADE

(BL)

the reviews, a soldier in the Second Massachusetts proudly proclaimed that the "Army of the Potomac is a collection of as fine troops . . . as there are in the world." An Ohioan seemed awestruck at such a magnificent display of the Republic's martial resources: "Such a great army! Thunder and lightning! The Johnnies could never whip this army!"

R. E. Lee and the Army of Northern Virginia prepared to meet their imposing foe after enduring a very difficult winter and early spring. Lee's own health remained uncertain. In early April he complained to his wife of "a good deal of pain in my chest, back, & arms." "Some fever remains," he added, and the doctors "have been tapping me all over like an old steam boiler before condemning it." By April 11, he reported himself much improved to his daughter Agnes: "I hope I shall recover my strength," he wrote, though his pulse stood at about 90, "too quick for an old man,"

according to his physicians.

The winter had forced hard choices on Lee. Unable to provision his cavalry, he had dispersed it widely to secure sufficient fodder. James Longstreet, head of the First Corps and Lee's senior lieutenant, also had been detached from the army with the divisions of Major General George E. Pickett and Major General John Bell Hood. Posted in Southside Virginia near Suffolk, Longstreet's soldiers foraged on a grand scale and stood ready to block Federal thrusts from Norfolk or the coast of North Carolina. Lee retained the divisions of Major General Richard H. Anderson and Major General Lafayette McLaws from Longstreet's corps, and Stonewall Jackson's entire Second Corps—the divisions of Major General Ambrose Powell Hill, Brigadier General Robert E. Rodes, Major General Jubal A. Early, and Brigadier General Raleigh E. Colston—stood ready to take the field against Hooker. Lee's artillery counted 220 guns, and approximately 2,500 Confederate cavalrymen were near at hand. The Army of Northern Virginia could muster slightly fewer than 61,000 men in all—which meant it would face an enemy more than twice its strength.

Superb leadership partially offset this daunting disparity in numbers. Lee's record

IN APRIL 1863, PRESIDENT LINCOLN TRAVELED TO STAFFORD COUNTY TO REVIEW THE ARMY. HERE, BRIGADIER GENERAL JOHN BUFORD'S CAVALRY DIVISION PASSES IN REVIEW.

(HW)

since June 1862 justified his reputation as an unexcelled field commander. He had forged an unshakable bond with his soldiers, and many Confederate civilians already viewed him as the personification of their war effort. "Like [George] Washington, he is a wise man, and a good man," noted a Georgia newspaper in late 1862, "and possesses in an eminent degree those qualities which are indispensable in the great leader and champion upon whom the country rests its hopes of present success and future independence." Stonewall Jackson stood second only to Lee in the estimation of the Confederate people (in Europe he probably was more famous) and inspired similar confidence among his men. As superior and loyal subordinate, Lee and Jackson formed a partnership that accounted for much of the army's success. Major General James E. B. "Jeb" Stuart complemented Lee and Jackson beautifully. He brought unmatched skill in the arts of gathering intelligence and screening the army to his work with the cavalry—talents that would prove crucial in the upcoming campaign. Finally, the Confederate artillery boasted a group of highly intelligent, innovative, and cocky young officers who benefited from a recent reorganization that placed Southern batteries in battalions. Unlike their opponents, Confederate gunners would be able to bring several batteries to bear on different sectors of the battlefield—a tactic that diminished Union advantages in firepower and quality of ordnance.

Splendid Confederate morale brightened the prospects for Southern success. Lee's soldiers had overcome long odds in winning spectacular victories, and they believed their generals would place them

in a position to do so again. Stephen Dodson Ramseur, a youthful brigadier in Robert Rodes's division, spoke for many in the army when he confidently stated that the "vandal hordes of the Northern Tyrant are struck down with terror arising from their past experience. They have learned to their sorrow that this army is made up of veterans equal to those of the 'Old Guard' of Napoleon." When Hooker seemed loath to advance during one spell of dry weather in March, Ramseur confidently attributed it to Fighting Joe's desire "to postpone the day of his defeat and humiliation." Lee reciprocated this confidence, seeing in his soldiers the capacity to offset much of the North's substantial edge in men and matériel.

Hooker's preponderant strength carried with it the strategic initiative. Well aware of Burnside's costly failure to bludgeon his way through Lee's defenders at the battle of Fredericksburg, he entertained no thought of challenging entrenched Confederates head-on. His initial plan

Splendid Confederate morale brightened the prospects for Southern success. Lee's soldiers had overcome long odds in winning spectacular victories, and they believed their generals would place them in a position to do so again.

The cavalry's turning march, begun promisingly enough on April 13, quickly slowed to a halt when heavy rains turned the Rappahannock into a frothing, impassable torrent. Only a single brigade made it across the river before the water rose precipitately and prompted Stoneman to abort the effort. "I greatly fear it is another failure already," an anguished Lincoln commented when Hooker explained Stoneman's problems. The president, Secretary of War Edwin M. Stanton, and General Halleck joined Hooker at Aquia on April 19 to discuss strategy.

called for turning Lee's left flank with the Cavalry Corps. Stoneman would take his command across the Rappahannock well upstream from Fredericksburg, after which the troopers would strike south and southeast to disrupt communications and transportation in Lee's rear. Expecting Lee to withdraw toward the Confederate capital in the face of this threat, Hooker would push his infantry over the Rappahannock and pursue the fleeing Rebels. "I have concluded that I will have more chance of inflicting a heavier blow upon the enemy by turning his position to my right," the general informed President Lincoln on April 11, "and, if practicable, to sever his connections with Richmond with my dragoon force and such light batteries as it may be deemed advisable to send with them." The next day Hooker urged Stoneman to remember that "celerity, audacity, and resolution are everything in war," pointedly telling the cavalryman that "on you and your noble command must depend in a great measure the extent and brilliancy of our success."

Hooker greeted his visitors with plans for a more ambitious turning operation. Stoneman's role remained essentially the same, but now Federal infantry would march simultaneously with their mounted comrades. While the Cavalry Corps crossed the river and began its dash into the Virginia interior, the 42,000 men of the Eleventh, Twelfth, and Fifth corps would move upriver, past well-defended Banks and United States fords, to negotiate the Rappahannock at Kelly's Ford. Once on the Rebel side of the river, they would hasten south to cross the Rapidan River at Germanna and Ely's fords, proceed into a heavily wooded area known as the Wilderness of Spotsylvania, concentrate at a crossroads called Chancellorsville, and then strike Lee's army from the west. Meanwhile, two divisions from Couch's Second Corps—another 10,000 men— would proceed to United States Ford and wait for Meade's Fifth Corps, marching east toward Lee, to drive Confederate defenders away from the river.

Hooker hoped to hold Lee's attention at Fredericksburg by shifting the Sixth and First corps, 40,000 strong and under John Sedgwick's overall command, to the Rebel side of the Rappahannock below town. Sedgwick's troops would threaten an attack against Stonewall Jackson's divisions holding the Confederate right flank. Further to mask Hooker's turning movement, Daniel Sickles's Third Corps and one division of the Second Corps, which together mustered nearly 25,000 muskets, would remain in their camps at Falmouth in plain view of watching Confederates.

If Hooker's grand design were to work, the three corps in the turning column should break clear of the Wilderness as quickly as possible. Covering approximately seventy square miles, the Wilderness extended south from the Rappahannock and Rapidan rivers with irregular borders running some three miles south and two miles east of Chancellorsville. Few roads traversed this gloomy forest, and only a handful of farms broke its dismal hold on the countryside. No longer dominated by mature growth, it was an ugly, scrub wasteland repeatedly

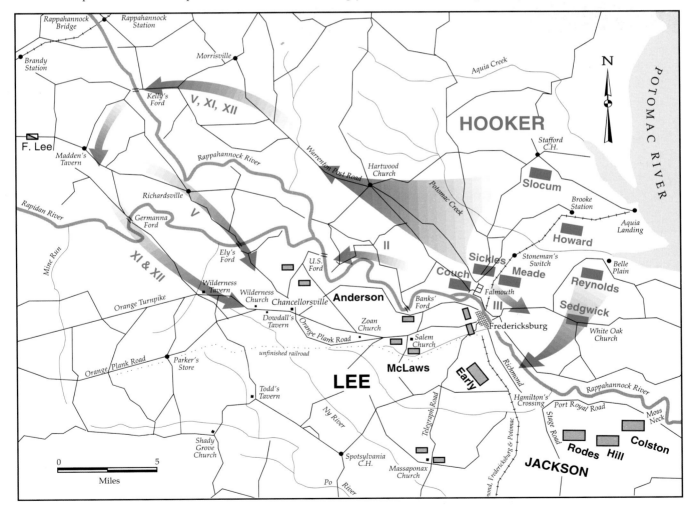

THE CAMPAIGN BEGINS: APRIL 27-30
Reynolds and Sedgwick cross the Rappahannock River below Fredericksburg to hold the Confederate army in place while Hooker leads the Fifth, Eleventh, and Twelfth Corps across Kelly's Ford, above town, effectively flanking Lee's Fredericksburg defenses. Sickles supports the Union army's right wing, while Couch sends two divisions of the Second Corps to U.S. Ford as a diversion.

cut over to feed hungry little iron furnaces in the region. Dense underbrush, choking vines, thickets of blackjack and hickory, and spindly saplings posed wicked obstacles to the passage of troops and would nullify to a large degree the superior Federal artillery. Just a few miles east of Chancellorsville the Wilderness gave way to open country where Northern numbers and equipment could have full weight. That was where the turning column should seek its outnumbered and outgunned enemy.

Efficient execution of the Union plan would squeeze Lee between powerful forces in front and rear while Stoneman's cavalry wreaked havoc on Confederate

lines of communication and supply. Hooker believed his opponent must either retreat, to be hounded by a pursuing Army of the Potomac, or attack the Federals on unfavorable ground. Either scenario promised victory sweeping enough to lay to rest the troubling ghosts of Fredericksburg and other Union failures against Lee. An admiring Porter Alexander awarded Hooker's design high marks: "On the whole I think this plan was decidedly the best strategy conceived in any of the campaigns ever set on foot against us," he wrote in his memoirs. "And the execution of it was, also, excellently managed, up to the morning of May 1st."

Initial execution of the plan was

splendid. Three Federal corps marched upriver on April 27, got across the Rappahannock and Rapidan with minimal delays, and by late afternoon of April 30 clustered near Chancellorsville. Couch's two divisions hurried to join them—having crossed the Rappahannock at United States Ford when Confederates on the right bank of the river withdrew in response to reports of heavy enemy activity to the west. Back at Fredericksburg, Union pontoons were in place by dawn on April 29, allowing thousands of Sedgwick's infantry to move into position opposite Lee's lines below the town. Musketry and artillery fire soon echoed along the river, continuing through the balance of that day and the next.

Many Union soldiers sensed that they had stolen a march on the crafty Lee. On the afternoon of April 30, George Meade shed his usual restraint to greet Henry Slocum at Chancellorsville with unabashed enthusiasm: "This is splendid, Slocum; hurrah for old Joe; we are on Lee's flank, and he does not know it. You take the Plank Road toward Fredericksburg, and I'll take the Pike, or vice versa, as you prefer, and we'll get out of this Wilderness."

Meade alluded to the major east-west routes through the Wilderness—the Orange Plank Road and the Orange Turnpike, both of which connected Orange Court House and Fredericksburg. The turnpike and plank road entered the area on separate beds but came together at Wilderness Church west of Chancellorsville to form a single road. They diverged again at Chancellorsville, with the plank road veering sharply southeast, only to rejoin the turnpike just east of Zoan Church for the last few miles to Fredericksburg. Unnamed by Meade, the River Road provided a third route to the rear of Lee's position along the

Rappahannock, angling northeast from Chancellorsville to trace a large arc on its way to the town. These three avenues lay open to the Federal flanking forces on the afternoon of April 30, but there would be no more marching that day. At 2:15 P.M., Hooker dispatched instructions from Federal headquarters at Falmouth for the elements of the turning column to halt at Chancellorsville, where he would join them that night.

Hooker arrived at Chancellorsville between 5:00 and 6:00 P.M. He found not a town or village but a rather imposing

country residence. Begun in the early nineteenth century by the Chancellor family, the building had been enlarged several times, functioning as an inn on the turnpike for many years. Traffic had decreased markedly by 1860, and the Chancellors then used the structure, which they called Chancellorsville, as a family home. The rambling brick house would serve as head-

WHILE HOOKER'S MAIN FORCE CROSSED THE RAPPAHANNOCK UPRIVER FROM FREDERICKSBURG, SOLDIERS OF THE FIRST AND SIXTH CORPS CROSSED ON PONTOON BRIDGES BELOW THE TOWN.

(HW)

"O THE HORROR OF THAT DAY!"

Although its name implies that it was a village, Chancellorsville was actually nothing more than a large brick house with a few scattered dependencies set in the heart of the Wilderness. The building was constructed by the Chancellor family in the early 1800s as an inn to accommodate travelers using the Orange Turnpike, and Frances Chancellor and her family were living at the house in 1863, when Joe Hooker occupied it as his headquarters. For two days Mrs. Chancellor, her chil-dren, and a few other local people remained sheltered in the house while the battle raged around them. But on May 3 Confederate artillery shells set the building on fire, compelling those inside to flee for safety. Sue Chancellor, then an eleven-year-old girl, described the arrival of the Union army at her home and the battle that followed. The Union officer she mentions was Lieutenant Colonel (later General) Joseph Dickinson of Hooker's staff.

"There were in the house my mother, her six daughters, her half-grown son, Miss Kate F, Aunt Nancy, and a little negro girl left by her mother when she went away to the Yankees. We put on all the clothes we could, and my sis-ters fastened securely in their hoop skirts the spoons and forks and pieces of the silver tea service which the engineers had given my mother . . . . Other valuables were secreted as best they could be. Presently the Yankees began to come, and they said that Chancellors-ville was to be General Hooker's headquarters, and we must all go into one room at the back of the house. They took all our comfortable rooms for themselves, while we slept on pallets on the floor . . . . General Hooker did not come until the next day. He paid no attention to my mother, but walked in and gave his orders. We never sat down to a meal again in that house, but they brought food to us in our room. If we attempted to go out, we were ordered back. We heard cannonading, but did not know where it was. We were joined by our neighbors, who fled or were brought to Chancellorsville house for refuge, until there were sixteen

quarters for the Army of the Potomac. Before departing for Chancellorsville (but after issuing his orders halting the turning column), Hooker had transmitted a con-gratulatory message: "It is with heartfelt satisfaction," he stated, "the commanding general announces to the army that the operations of the last three days have determined that our enemy must either ingloriously fly, or come out from behind his defenses and give us battle on our own ground, where certain destruction awaits him."

Once at the crossroads, Hooker brimmed with confidence. Sickles's Third Corps would join the turning column early the next morning. The commanding gener-al would then oversee an advance he believed certain to unnerve the previously unflappable R. E. Lee. Within earshot of a newspaper correspondent, Hooker stated, "The rebel army is now the legitimate property of the Army of the Potomac. They may as well pack up their haversacks and make for Richmond. I shall be after them."

Lee's position did seem nearly hope-less. Caught between the hammer of the flanking force at Chancellorsville and women and children in that room. From the windows we could see couriers coming and going and knew that the troops were cutting down trees and throwing up breastworks. I know now that they were pretty well satisfied with their position and were confident of victory.

Well, we got through Thursday and Friday as best we could, but on Saturday, the 2d of May, the firing was much nearer, and General Hooker ordered us to be taken to the basement. The house was full of wounded. They had taken our sitting room as an operating room and our piano as an amputating table. One of the surgeons came to my mother and said, 'There are two wounded Rebels here, and if you wish you can attend to them,' which she did.

There was water in the basement over our shoetops, and one of the surgeons brought my mother down a bottle of whisky and told her that we should all take some, which we did, with the exception of Aunt Nancy, who said: 'No sah, I ain't gwine tek it; I might git pizened.'

There was firing and fighting, and they were bringing in the wounded all that day; but I must say that they did not forget to bring us some food. It was late that day when the awful time began. Cannonading on all sides and such shrieks and groans, such commotion of all kinds! We thought that we were frightened before, but this was beyond everything and kept up until after dark. Upstairs they were bringing in the wounded, and we could hear their screams of pain. This was Jackson's flank movement, but we did not know it then. Again we spent the night, sixteen of us, in that one room, the last night in the old house.

Early in the morning they came for us to go into the cellar, and in passing through the upper porch I saw how the chairs were riddled with bullets and the shattered columns which had fallen and injured General Hooker. O the horror of that day! The piles of legs and arms outside the sitting room window and the rows and rows of dead bodies covered with canvas! The fighting was awful, and the frightened men crowded into the basement for protection from the deadly fire of the Confederates, but an officer came and ordered them out, commanding them not to intrude upon the terrorstricken women. Presently down the steps the same officer came precipitously and bade us get out at once, 'For madam, the house is on fire, but I will see that you are protected and taken to a place of safety.' This was Gen. Joseph Dickinson. . . . Cannon were booming and missiles of death were flying in every direction as this terrified band of women and children came stumbling out of the cellar. If anybody thinks that a battle is an orderly attack of rows of men, I can tell them differently, for I have been there.

The sight that met our eyes as we came out of the dim light of that basement beggars description. The woods around the house were a sheet of fire, the air was filled with shot and shell, horses were running, rearing, and screaming, the men, a mass of confusion, moaning, cursing, and praying. They were bringing the wounded out of the house, as it was on fire in several places. . . . Slowly we picked our way over the bleeding bodies of the dead and wounded, General Dickinson riding ahead, my mother walking alongside with her hand on his knee, I clinging close to her, and the others following behind. At the last look our old home was completely enveloped in flames.

> *"The woods around the house were a sheet of fire, the air was filled with shot and shell, horses were running, rearing, and screaming, the men, a mass of confusion, moaning, cursing, and praying."*

Sedgwick's solid anvil at Fredericksburg, his best option might be to slip southward in search of a better tactical situation. But as so often in the past, the Confederate chieftain opted for a daringly unpredictable response. Jeb Stuart's hardworking troopers—free to roam the flanks of the army because so many of Stoneman's cavalrymen had ridden southward—supplied intelligence on April 29 about Federal crossings at Kelly's Ford and enemy columns moving toward the fords on the Rapidan. That evening Lee ordered Richard H. Anderson to go to Chancellorsville and

RESPONSIBILITY FOR GUARDING THE FORDS ABOVE FREDERICKSBURG FELL TO DICK ANDERSON. WHEN UNION TROOPS CROSSED BEYOND HIS LEFT FLANK, ANDERSON FELL BACK TO ZOAN CHURCH.

(BL)

instructed Lafayette McLaws to prepare his division to follow. Anderson reached his destination about midnight to find Brigadier General William Mahone's and Brigadier General Carnot Posey's brigades, which had fallen back from United States Ford earlier in the day. Apprised that a heavy force of Union infantry was bearing down on the crossroads—and under orders from Lee "to select a good line and fortify it strongly"—Anderson withdrew to a ridge just beyond the eastern edge of the Wilderness. This position, near a small Baptist church with the unusual name Zoan, covered the plank road, the turnpike, and the Old Mine or Mountain Road that linked the turnpike with United States Ford. Soon reinforced by a third of his brigades, Brigadier General Ambrose R. Wright's Georgians, Anderson ordered the men to

dig in. Their efforts created some of the first field fortifications constructed by the Army of Northern Virginia.

Through a tense April 29 and into the next day, Lee watched Union movements at Fredericksburg and pondered intelligence about activity upriver. Hooker had kept him off balance since February, when he had confessed to Mrs. Lee his inability to fathom the Federal commander's intentions: "I owe Mr. F. J. Hooker no thanks for keeping me here in this state of expectancy. He ought to have made up his mind long ago what to do." Uncertainty ended on April 30 when Lee decided that Sedgwick intended nothing more than a facade of aggressiveness at Fredericksburg. "It was now apparent that the main attack would be made upon our flank and rear," Lee later explained. "It was therefore determined to leave sufficient troops to hold our lines [at Fredericksburg], and with the main body of the army to give battle to the approaching column."

How would Lee divide his small army? To keep an eye on Sedgwick, Jubal Early would remain at Fredericksburg with his division from Jackson's Second Corps, Brigadier General William Barksdale's brigade of Mississippians from McLaws's

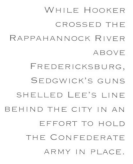

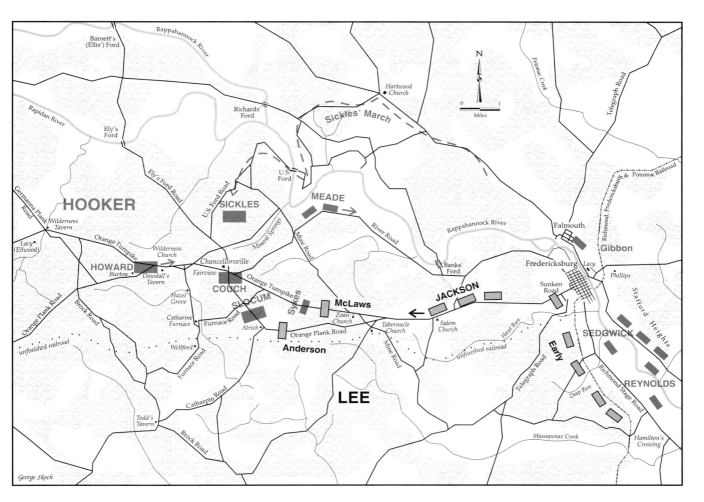

LEE ACCEPTS HOOKER'S CHALLENGE: MAY 1
Lee reacts to Hooker's opening move by boldly dividing his army. He sends Jackson's corps to reinforce McLaws and Anderson at Zoan Church, while leaving Early to hold the Fredericksburg line against Reynolds, Sedgwick, and Gibbon. The Confederates attack Sykes's division on the Orange Turnpike and are about to come to grips with Slocum's corps on the Orange Plank Road when Hooker orders the Union army to withdraw to Chancellorsville.

division, and roughly one-quarter of the army's artillery—a total of 9,000 soldiers and 56 guns. The rest of the Second Corps would march westward to join Anderson and McLaws for a showdown with Hooker's main body.

Jackson's infantry and artillery were on the move under a memorably bright moon before dawn on Friday, May 1. With adrenaline pumping in anticipation of battle, the Confederates devoured the miles separating them from their blue-clad enemy. Jackson arrived at Anderson's position near Zoan Church by 8:00 A.M. McLaws's brigades had preceded them by a

few hours. The men at Zoan who greeted Jackson assumed they would be fighting on the defensive, but they soon discovered that Stonewall harbored only offensive thoughts. Orders swiftly revealed his intention—Mahone's brigade and McLaws's division would move west on the turnpike, while Anderson's other brigades, supported by Jackson's arriving men, would push toward Chancellorsville on the plank road. By eleven o'clock the Confederates were in motion. A Confederate artillerist, watching Jackson's infantry pour westward, recalled the scene as Lee joined Jackson to observe

the developing action: "Up the road from Fredericksburg comes marching a dense & swarming column of our shabby gray ranks, and at the head of them rode both General Lee & Stonewall Jackson. . . . We were not going to wait for the enemy to come & attack us . . . we were going out on the warpath after him." The presence of Lee and Jackson, he added, "meant that it was to be a supreme effort, a union of audacity & desperation."

Joseph Hooker also entertained offensive thoughts on the morning of May 1. A beautiful day beckoned. Light breezes played among the army's uncased

banners, and the men sensed important work ahead. Many officers had been unhappy with Hooker's decision to bivouac the turning column near Chancellorsville instead of moving on during the afternoon and evening of April 30. Now they heard with relief that the army would seek to regain its forward momentum. With 70,000 soldiers and 184 guns on hand, Hooker ordered a three-pronged advance toward Fredericksburg. George Meade took two divisions of his Fifth Corps out the River Road and sent Major General George Sykes's division, which boasted two brigades of U.S. Regulars, east on the turnpike. Farther south, Slocum's Twelfth Corps filled the plank road, with Howard's Eleventh Corps in close support. Couch's divisions, soon to be reinforced by the Third Corps then crossing United States Ford, would stand in reserve. Hooker envisioned a rapid march to take his troops out of the Wilderness, seize control of the ridge at Zoan Church, and permit him to stage a final strike against Fredericksburg.

Headed toward each other on the same roads, thousands of Federals and Confederates rapidly approached an inevitable collision. On the plank road, a captain in Slocum's corps instinctively looked at his watch when he noticed the

first shell burst: "Twenty minutes past eleven," he remarked. "The first gun of the battle of Chancellorsville." Fighting soon flared along the turnpike and plank road—and almost immediately illuminated a stark contrast in leadership. Stonewall Jackson urged his men forward, directing new units to either the turnpike or plank road and seeking to press the enemy. Back at Chancellorsville, Hooker shrank from the prospect of battle, issuing instructions at 2:00 P.M. for his corps commanders to suspend their advances and fall back to the crossroads.

The decisive moment of the campaign had arrived. Hooker's troops on the turnpike were nearing the vital ridge at Zoan Church. Slocum's units had made similar progress on the plank road. From the Zoan high ground eastward the landscape steadily descended toward

Fredericksburg and the Rappahannock. Possession of the ridge would open the way to possible victory. But Hooker pulled his soldiers off the rising ground, back into the clutching forest. With every yard his soldiers trod into the woods, Hooker relinquished a measure of his numerical superiority. He had come face to face with R. E. Lee and had lost his nerve. In effect, the Chancellorsville campaign ended on the morning of May 1 because Hooker lacked the will to commit his army to a decisive confrontation with Lee. Much hard fighting lay ahead. Thousands of men would be killed or maimed, but any real hope for Union victory slowly receded as puzzled Federal veterans retreated away from the bright sunlight into the Wilderness.

Some of Hooker's subordinates reacted angrily. Slocum's report for the campaign implicitly criticized the commanding general by noting that the Twelfth Corps was gaining ground and had lost just ten men when the order to retreat arrived. On the River Road, Meade had encountered only the lightest opposition in reaching a point within sight of Banks Ford. Possession of that vital crossing would greatly shorten the distance between the two wings of Hooker's army. But Hooker's orders allowed no discretion. Grudgingly reversing direction, Meade betrayed frustration and wrath: "My God," he exclaimed, "if we can't hold the top of a hill, we certainly can't hold the bottom of it!"

By mid-afternoon Hooker's troops had begun entrenching along a defensive line centered on Chancellorsville. They originally deployed north to south facing east, but shortly after Hooker's order to withdraw Federals detected a threat on their right flank about a mile south of the plank road. A. R. Wright's Georgians had

Much hard fighting lay ahead. Thousands of men would be killed or maimed, but any real hope for Union victory slowly receded as puzzled Federal veterans retreated away from the bright sunlight into the Wilderness.

Wilderness Church and also facing south. Sickles's troops, who had arrived about noon, boosted the number of men under Hooker's direct control.

Lee's army was arrayed to the east and southeast, its advance units within a mile of Chancellorsville. McLaws's brigades straddled the turnpike, while Anderson's and Jackson's divisions deployed along the plank road. Musketry and cannon fire died away as evening came on. Another bright moon "filled the heavens with light," noted a South Carolinian, casting weird shadows in the forest. A damp chill settled over the Wilderness, the night's silence broken by the axes of Union pioneers laboring to strengthen Hooker's works.

Although thoroughly beaten mentally, Hooker maintained his outward bravado. He told Couch that Lee was "just where I want him; he must fight me on my own ground." But neither Couch nor others at Federal headquarters doubted the magnitude of the day's lost opportunity. "The retrograde movement had prepared me for something of the kind," Couch later wrote of Hooker's hollow claims, "but to hear from his own lips that the advantages gained by the successful marches of his lieutenants were to culminate in fighting a defensive battle in that nest of thickets was too much." Couch left Hooker's presence "with the belief that my commanding general was a whipped man." Late that afternoon Federal corps chiefs at Chancellorsville received a prophetic message from Hooker: "The major general commanding trusts that a suspension in the attack to-day will embolden the enemy to attack him."

deployed in the bed of an unfinished railroad that roughly paralleled the plank road and turnpike, following it west through the woods and forcing the Federals to readjust. Hooker drew his new line to protect against Confederates to the south and east. Shaped like a broad, flat V with the apex near Chancellorsville, it consisted of Meade's corps and Couch's two divisions on the left, anchored on the Rappahannock and facing east and southeast; Slocum's corps in the center facing south; and Howard's corps holding the right along the turnpike, extending past

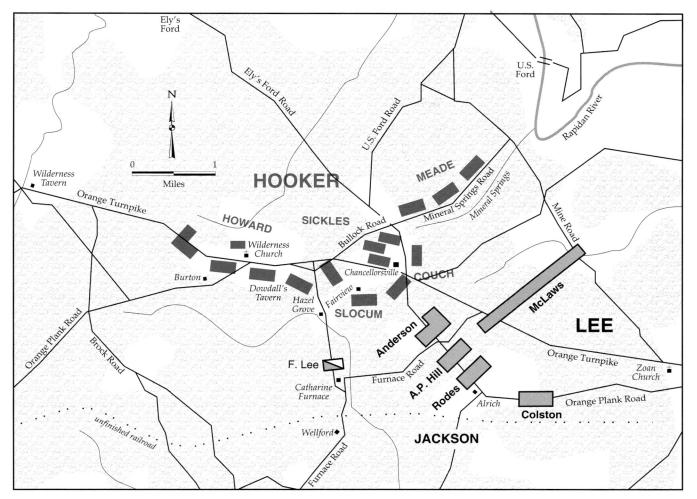

SITUATION: MAY 1, NIGHT
Hooker falls back to a tight defensive line around Chancellorsville. Meade holds a position on the river, Couch and
Slocum occupy the center of the line, and Howard's corps stretches west out the Orange Turnpike. Sickles is in reserve
at Chancellorsville. Lee, meanwhile, moves up and occupies the ridge abandoned by Hooker earlier in the day.

The initiative had passed to Lee—of all Confederate generals the one most likely to attack a vacillating enemy. The Army of Northern Virginia remained in a perilous situation, lodged between Hooker and Sedgwick. Lee and Jackson met that night where a narrow lane from Catharine Furnace intersected the plank road about a mile southeast of Hooker's headquarters. They sat on cracker boxes abandoned by the retreating Yankees, light from a modest fire flickering in the damp air. How could they get at the enemy? Lee had ridden toward the Union left during the afternoon and found no opening. Rough ground, numerous Federals, and an absence of roads rendered that Union flank safe.

Confederate engineering officers reconnoitered the enemy's center and reported it also too strong to assail. Reports from various sources—including Brigadier General Fitzhugh Lee of Stuart's cavalry, various staff officers, and local residents—suggested that Hooker's right might be vulnerable. If enough infantry could move undetected across Hooker's front and hit the exposed flank, Lee might forge a decisive victory. Key information about possible routes for the flank march came from Charles Beverly Wellford, a veteran of Lee's army now overseeing Catharine Furnace (a Wellford enterprise named for the family's matriarch), Jackson's gifted cartographer Jedediah Hotchkiss, and Beverly Tucker

Lacy, a clergyman with Jackson whose brother lived in the area.

Lee decided in the early hours of May 2 on a breathtakingly dangerous gamble. He would divide his outnumbered army for a second time, sending 28,000 men of Jackson's Second Corps around Hooker's front to launch an attack on the Union right flank. With the brigades under Anderson and McLaws—roughly 13,000 men supported by 24 guns—Lee would strive to occupy Hooker's attention until Jackson got into position. Should Hooker discover Lee's intention, the Federals could crush the pieces of the Army of Northern Virginia in detail (Jubal Early's small force remained outnumbered about four to one at Fredericksburg). Doubtless aware of that grim possibility, Lee and Jackson discussed the path the Second Corps would take. Lee would leave all details of the movement to Jackson. Illustrating by graphic example of what he hoped to achieve, Lee chose a moment to align a batch of broomstraws on a box—then brushed them to the ground. The generals parted just before dawn on May 2. Lee would see to the demonstration in front of Hooker while Jackson started his divisions on a march that would culminate in the Civil War's most famous flank attack.

Jackson's column was in motion between seven and eight o'clock. Its twelve-mile route would follow the Catharine Furnace Road to the ironworks, continuing southwest to the junction with the Brock Road. Turning left at that point, the men would march a few hundred yards south before turning right onto a narrow woods road that eventually deposited them back onto the Brock Road, which in turn would take them to the plank road. The plan called for the attack to proceed east along the plank road. Jackson rode near the front of Rodes's division, which led the march. Colston's and then Hill's commands stretched out behind. Brigadier General Alfred H. Colquitt's brigade of Georgians had the honor of leading the march. At about eight o'clock, the first of Jackson's infantry passed Lee's bivouac on their way toward the furnace. "Old Jack" reined in his sorrel to have a few quiet words with Lee. He gestured toward Catharine Furnace, Lee nodded, and Jackson took his leave. Lee never saw his redoubtable lieutenant again.

Hours of hard work and anxiety lay ahead for Lee. He helped place the soldiers of Anderson and McLaws, watched carefully for Hooker's reaction, and wondered about Jackson's progress and Jubal Early's situation at Fredericksburg. The Confederate line fronting Hooker eventually extended three and one-half miles from near Catharine Furnace on the southwest, where Carnot Posey's brigade was posted, northwest across the plank road and the turnpike to the Old Mine Road. Only seven brigades strong, this force feigned numerous attacks. Individual regiments frequently deployed huge numbers of skirmishers to create the illusion of greater numbers. Federals easily repulsed the Confederate feints but never followed up with counterattacks. Lee knew his thin line could resist no serious northern advance. "It is plain that if the enemy is too strong for me here," he informed Jefferson Davis, "I shall have to fall back, and Fredericksburg must be abandoned." Lee also told the president about the flank march: "I am now swinging around to my left to come up in his [Hooker's] rear."

Jackson's men trod on narrow paths damp and soft enough for easy marching. Cavalry preceded the infantry and screened the right flank. Each division marched with its artillery, ambulances, and ammunition trains behind it. From head to tail the column stretched ten miles. Four hours elapsed between the time the first and last brigades passed Lee's bivouac. Jackson hoped to maintain his usual pace of one mile every twenty-five minutes with a ten-minute break each hour. Pleasantly cool under clear skies when the movement began, the temperature climbed steadily as the day wore on. Colonel Charles T. Zachry of the Twenty-Seventh Georgia, a regiment in Colquitt's brigade, remarked six days later that "the march was a trying one for the men; the day was very warm; many fell out of ranks exhausted, some fainting and having spasms."

Noted for prodigious marching in the Shenandoah Valley and elsewhere, Jackson's famous "foot cavalry" would consume the entire day reaching its jump-off point and forming for the assault. Why did it take so long? One observer explained: "Every little inequality of ground, & every mud hole, especially if the road be narrow, causes a column to string out & lose distance. So that, though the head may advance steadily, the rear has to alternately halt & start, & halt & start, in the most heartbreaking way, wearing out the men and consuming precious daylight, often beyond the calculations even of experienced soldiers."

So many Confederates on so long a march invited detection. Scarcely a mile beyond Lee's bivouac, the column became visible to Federals a mile and a quarter northwest on the high plateau called Hazel Grove. Brigadier General David Bell Birney's division of Sickles's corps held Hazel Grove, and at about 8:00 A.M. Birney informed Sickles "that a continuous column

JACKSON'S INFANTRY SENSED THAT THEY WERE HEADED AROUND THE UNION ARMY, AND IT PUT THEM IN HIGH SPIRITS. "TELL OLD JACK WE'RE ALL A-COMING," THEY JOKED TO PASSING STAFF OFFICERS. "DON'T LET HIM BEGIN THE FUSS TILL WE GIT THAR!"

(BL)

ENGRAVINGS LIKE THIS ONE TENDED TO PORTRAY BATTLES AS TIDY, WELL MANAGED AFFAIRS. SUE CHANCELLOR KNEW OTHERWISE. "IF ANYBODY THINKS THAT A BATTLE IS AN ORDERLY ATTACK OF ROWS OF MEN, I CAN TELL HIM DIFFERENTLY," SHE LATER ASSERTED.

(LC)

of infantry, trains, and ambulances was passing my front toward the right." Birney ordered the rifled pieces of Battery B, First New Jersey Artillery, to open fire on the Confederates, causing them to double-quick past the gap in the woods. Sickles subsequently rode to Hazel Grove to watch the passing Confederates. "The continuous column . . . was observed for three hours moving apparently in a southerly direction toward Orange Court-House," wrote Sickles in his report of the battle. "I hastened to report these movements through staff officers to the general-in-chief, and communicated the substance of them in the same manner to Major-General Howard, on my right, and also to Major-General Slocum, inviting their cooperation in case the general-in-chief should authorize me to follow up the enemy and attack his columns."

Shortly after nine o'clock, a courier from Birney found Hooker at the Chancellor house and explained about the Confederate column. Hooker had been up since before sunrise and already had examined his right flank. Troops had cheered as he rode by, and he remarked that the Union position seemed strong—which it was if Confederates attacked from the south. Alerted by Birney's message, Hooker scanned the area near Catharine Furnace through his fieldglasses. He caught glimpses of the Confederates in two places —the break in the woods where Birney had seen them and a section of the Furnace Road that ran south from the ironworks toward the Wellford house. Lee's men might be retreating, thought Hooker, but they also might be searching for an opening to strike the Union right flank. His morning inspection had revealed that Howard's line offered little strength facing west. In a dispatch dated 9:30 A.M., Hooker warned Howard to prepare for trouble from that direction: "We have good reason to suppose the enemy is moving to our right. Please advance your pickets for purposes of observation as far as may be safe in order to obtain timely information of their approach."

Although Howard later claimed this dispatch never reached him, he knew from other sources that Confederates might be marching toward his right. He informed Hooker at 10:50 A.M. about "a column of infantry moving westward on a road parallel with this [the turnpike] on a ridge about 1 1/2 to 2 m[iles] south of this." Howard assured his commander that he was "taking measures to resist an attack from the west." In fact, he did virtually nothing to rearrange his corps, the vast majority of which continued to face south along the turnpike.

While Howard contented himself with nominal adjustments to his line, Hooker remained cautious and Dan Sickles exuded a restless determination to strike the Rebels. Passing up the chance to launch a major assault against the enemy's column, Hooker did send discretionary orders for Sedgwick "to attack the enemy in his front" if "an opportunity presents itself with a reasonable expectation of success." Sickles received permission at noon "to advance cautiously toward the road followed by the enemy, and harass the movement as much as possible."

These instructions came too late to interfere with Jackson's main body. The trains, ambulances, and other vehicles accompanying the column had left the Furnace Road to follow alternate paths that carried them safely beyond Federal pressure at the ironworks. Jackson also had detached the Twenty-third Georgia of Colquitt's brigade to guard the rear of the column. The Georgians engaged elements of Birney's division and Colonel Hiram Berdan's sharpshooters near Catharine Furnace during the early afternoon. Driven south from the furnace, the Twenty-third made a stand just north of the Wellford house in a portion of the same unfinished railroad cut Wright's brigade had used the day before. The Federals finally overran this position about 5:00 P.M., capturing most of the defenders (Colonel Emory Fiske Best of the Twenty-third fled the cut and subsequently was court-martialed and convicted of cowardice). Two brigades from A. P. Hill's division, which had turned back to support Best's regiment and now deployed on an open plateau near the Wellford place, efficiently contained Sickles's success.

Most of Jackson's infantry marched on unaware that Sickles's troops nipped at the rear of their column. They reached the Brock Road—the principal north-south artery through that part of the Wilderness—and turned left as planned, crossed a pair of small ridges, then made a

right turn onto a narrow woods path that took them, four abreast, northward to a reunion with the Brock Road. A short distance more and they reached the junction of the Brock and Orange Plank roads. Here Jackson had envisioned turning east on the plank road to cover the final two miles before striking the enemy at Wilderness Church. Instead he found Fitzhugh Lee with exciting news. Taking Jackson east along the plank road, Lee ascended to high ground on the Burton farm whence he gestured toward a memorable sight: To their front, spread out along the turnpike, were thousands of Federal soldiers at rest. Arms stood stacked, and wisps of smoke from campfires climbed lazily skyward. No sign indicated any expectation of a Confederate assault from the west. Fitz Lee later recalled that Jackson's eyes "burned with a brilliant glow, lighting his sad face."

It was nearly 3:00 P.M. Much of the day already had been taken up by marching, but Jackson might achieve complete surprise if his column continued on to the turnpike before turning east. "Tell General

WILDERNESS CHURCH STOOD AT THE CENTER OF HOWARD'S LINE. CARL SCHURZ WOULD LATER FORM HIS DIVISION NEAR THE CHURCH, FACING WEST, IN AN EFFORT TO MEET JACKSON'S ATTACK.

(NPS)

JACKSON VIEWS THE UNION LINES

On May 2, 1863, Stonewall Jackson led his corps through the Wilderness toward the Union army's right flank, held by Major General Oliver O. Howard's Eleventh Corps. Jackson believed Howard's line ended near the Wilderness Church and therefore planned to make his attack up the Orange Plank Road. As he neared the plank road that afternoon, however, he met Major General Fitzhugh Lee, whose cavalry was screening his march. Lee asked Jackson to follow him down the plank road to the Burton farm, which stood on a knoll just half a mile from the Union line. There, Jackson saw that Howard's line actually extended a mile beyond the church, making an attack up the plank road impractical. Based on this information, he had his corps continue up the Brock Road to the Orange Turnpike, thereby placing it squarely on Howard's exposed flank. In a speech made sixteen years after the battle, Fitz Lee described his meeting with Jackson at the Burton farm:

"Jackson was marching on. My cavalry was well in his front. Upon reaching the Plank road, some five miles west of Chancellorsville, my command was halted, and while waiting for Jackson to come up, I made a personal reconnaissance to locate the Federal right for Jackson's attack. With one staff officer, I rode across and beyond the Plank road, in the direction of the Old turnpike, pursuing a path through the woods, momentarily expecting to find evidence of the enemy's presence. Seeing a wooded hill in the distance, I determined, if possible, to get upon its top, as it promised a view of the adjacent country. Cautiously I ascended its side, reaching the open spot upon its summit without molestation. What a sight presented itself before me! Below, and but a few hundred

yards distant, ran the Federal line of battle. I was in rear of Howard's right. There were the line of defence, with abatis in front, and long lines of stacked arms in rear. Two cannon were visible in the part of the line seen. The soldiers were in groups in the rear, laughing, chatting, smoking, probably engaged, here and there, in games of cards, and other amusements indulged in while feeling safe and comfortable, awaiting orders. In rear of them

FITZHUGH LEE

(BL)

were other parties driving up and butchering beeves. . . . So impressed was I with my discovery, that I rode rapidly back to the point on the Plank road where I had left my cavalry, and back down the road Jackson was moving until I met 'Stonewall' himself. 'General,' said I, 'if you will ride with me, halting your column here, out of sight, I will show you the enemy's right, and you will perceive the great advantage of attacking down the Old turn-

pike instead of the Plank road, the enemy's lines being taken in reverse. Bring only one courier, as you will be in view from the top of the hill.' Jackson assented, and I rapidly conducted him to the point of observation. There had been no change in the picture.

I only knew Jackson slightly. I watched him closely as he gazed upon Howard's troops. It was then about 2 P.M. His eyes burned with a brilliant glow, lighting up a sad face. His expression was one of intense interest, his face was colored slightly with the paint of approaching battle, and radiant at the success of his flank movement. . . . To the remarks made to him while the unconscious line of blue was pointed out, he did not reply once during the five minutes he was on the hill, and yet his lips were moving. From what I have read and heard of Jackson since that day, I know now what he was doing then. Oh! 'beware of rashness,' General Hooker. Stonewall Jackson is praying in full view and in rear of your right flank! . . .

'Tell General Rodes,' said he, suddenly whirling his horse towards the courier, 'to move across the Old plank-road; halt when he gets to the Old turnpike, and I will join him there.' One more look upon the Federal lines, and then he rode rapidly down the hill."

"His eyes burned with a brilliant glow, lighting up a sad face. His expression was one of intense interest, his face was colored slightly with the paint of approaching battle, and radiant at the success of his flank movement."

AFTER VIEWING THE UNION LINE FROM THE
BURTON FARM, JACKSON TOOK A MOMENT TO
SCRIBBLE THIS DISPATCH TO ROBERT E. LEE.
THREE HOURS LATER HE ATTACKED.

(BL)

Rodes to move across the Plank Road," he
snapped to a courier, "halt when he gets to
the old turnpike, and I will join him there."
Before riding to join his men, Jackson
scribbled a note to R. E. Lee: "I hope as
soon as practicable to attack. . . . The leading division is up and the next two appear
to be well closed."

Two additional miles brought the van
of Rodes's division to the turnpike. Brigade
after brigade turned east along that thor-
oughfare, forming in long lines that straddled the road facing east and extended
nearly a mile in each direction. Soon two
complete lines, separated by about 100
yards, and part of a third were in place.
Because the sun inexorably dipped toward
the western horizon, Jackson could not
wait for the last brigades of Hill's division
to arrive. Thousands of soldiers stood in

position to smash directly into the unpro-
tected right flank of O. O. Howard's
Eleventh Corps. Accounts vary as to the
precise time, but between 5:15 and
6:00 P.M. Jackson checked his watch,
then looked at Robert Rodes, the young
brigadier general whose troops manned
the front line. "Are you ready, General
Rodes?" asked Jackson. "Yes, sir," came the
steady reply. "You can go forward then."

Nearly 20,000 Confederates surged
forward through trees and underbrush. The
unnerving whoop of the Rebel Yell floated
through the forest, and a wave of terrified
animals rolled eastward in front of the
advancing human tide. Startled Federals at
first pointed and laughed as rabbits and
deer scattered through their lines—then
frantically sought to form when they realized why the beasts had burst from the
woods. Howard's men never had a chance.
Only five regiments faced the oncoming
Rebels. Confronting enemy lines that
far overlapped their own, they offered
token resistance before falling back in
disorder. Near Wilderness Church, Carl
Schurz shifted his division's alignment
from south to west.
"Round came his line
like a top, swinging
sharply as though
upon a pivot," wrote
an admiring Union
soldier of Schurz's
maneuver. "Not
more than two min-
utes before Schurz's
men were facing
south. Now their
front was to the
west—in unbroken
line, shoulder to
shoulder, to stem the

AT 5:15 P.M., OR
SHORTLY THEREAFTER,
ROBERT RODES
REPORTED HIS DIVISION
READY FOR ACTION.
"YOU CAN GO FORWARD
THEN," JACKSON
REPLIED.

(LC)

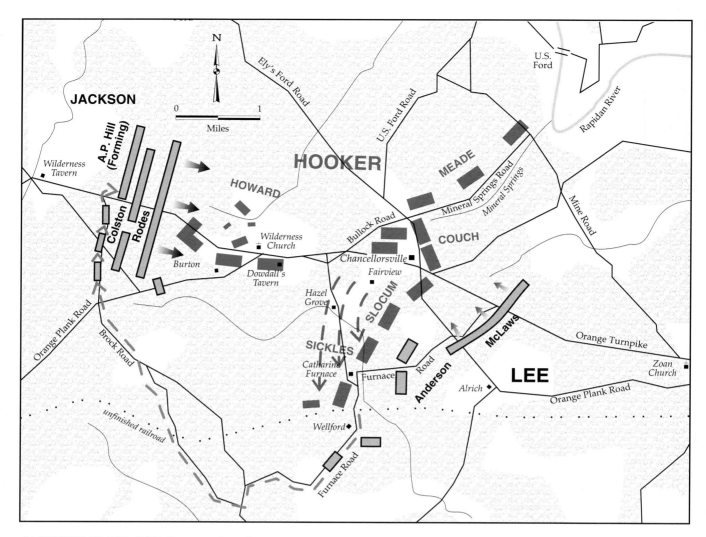

JACKSON'S FLANK ATTACK: MAY 2, 5-6 P.M.
While Lee spars with Hooker south and east of Chancellorsville, Jackson leads three divisions of the Second Corps on a daylight march around the Union army's right flank. Observing Jackson's march, Hooker sends Sickles to harass the Confederate column at Catharine Furnace and later orders Slocum forward as well. This isolates Howard's corps, which later folds under the weight of Jackson's afternoon assault.

torrent of men." Twenty minutes of hard fighting settled the issue. Flanked on both ends of his line, Schurz ordered a retreat at about 6:30 P.M. Other pockets of Federals also fought fiercely, and artillery Captain Hubert Dilger—called "Leather-breeches" because he affected doeskin trousers—heroically worked a cannon on the turnpike.

O. O. Howard's splendid behavior during the fighting partially redeemed his careless deployment. He seized a standard and shouted for his men to stand. Oblivious to minié balls that whizzed around him, he managed to rally small

knots of soldiers before witnessing the complete disintegration of his corps. "More quickly than it could be told," he sadly observed, "with all the fury of the wildest hailstorm, everything, every sort of organization that lay in the path of the mad current of panic-stricken men had to give way and be broken into fragments."

Eleventh Corps resistance had collapsed by about 7:00 P.M. Several thousand of Howard's men collected over the next hour at Fairview, a large clearing across the plank road from Chancellorsville. Captain Clermont L. Best, chief of artillery in the Twelfth Corps, massed 37 guns at

Fairview and directed an effective fire westward toward the advancing Confederates. Rodes's division, badly disorganized in victory, halted at 7:15 near a set of abandoned works that Slocum's soldiers had erected across the plank road roughly a mile west of Chancellorsville. Soon to be excoriated as the "damned Dutchmen" who fled rather than fighting Jackson's veterans, the Eleventh Corps had performed reasonably well under the circumstances. Nearly 2,500 casualties (roughly 25 percent of its strength), among them a dozen of twenty-three regimental commanders, attested to its efforts.

Joseph Hooker had roused himself from a curious lethargy to assist in stabilizing the Union line west of Chancellorsville. He and members of his staff vainly sought to stem the tide of fugitives pouring east along the plank road. At one point, Hooker encouraged Major General Hiram G. Berry, who led the Third Corps division the commanding general himself had organized nineteen months earlier, to "throw your men into the breach—receive the enemy on your bayonets—don't fire a shot—they can't see you." Berry's men went into line perpendicular to the plank road a half mile west of Chancellorsville

about the time Jackson's attack lost momentum.

The Confederate assault might have accomplished a great deal more. Alfred Colquitt, a Georgia politician whose brigade occupied the right of the first line of attackers, ignored Jackson's stern orders to move ahead without regard to his flanks. Imagining a Union threat from the south, Colquitt halted his brigade after a brief time, in the process stacking up Dodson Ramseur's fine brigade of North Carolinians in the second line as well as the Stonewall Brigade, which was attempting to move east along the plank road. Five thousand Confederates remained stationary while a furious Ramseur demand-ed to know why. Colquitt finally moved on, leaving Ramseur to search in vain for the phantom enemy. Ramseur subsequently reported that "not a solitary Yankee was to be seen" where the rattled Georgian had concocted a Federal menace.

Night enveloped a chaotic field. The moon rose over the Wilderness to create a fantastic landscape of shadows broken by shafts of light. The men of Rodes and Colston, "mingled together in inextricable confusion" during the attack, would have to be sorted out. Hill's brigades made their way to the front. The Eleventh Corps lay scattered over several miles, and thousands of its soldiers would not be available for further service for many hours. Third Corps units involved in the fighting at Catharine Furnace and the Wellford house found themselves isolated from the main Union position and struggled to link up with comrades along the plank road and at Chancellorsville.

By 9:00 P.M., Sickles's men had settled into position at Hazel Grove facing north-west. To their right, Brigadier General Alpheus S. Williams's division of Slocum's corps extended the line to the plank road. Its right touched the left of Berry's division, positioned north of the plank road and, like Williams's command, facing west. Other units of the Second and Twelfth corps were spread around the Chancellorsville crossroads. The Fifth Corps line angled from a position just north of Chancellorsville toward Scott's Dam on the Rappahannock, and the divisions of John Reynolds's First Corps, which had begun the day on the Confederate side of the river at Fredericksburg, were slowly making their way from United States Ford to Chancellorsville. Between 11:00 P.M. and midnight, Sickles mount-ed a groping assault from Hazel Grove toward the

plank road during which his men came under artillery and musket fire from the Twelfth Corps. "I have no information as to the damage suffered by our troops from our own fire," confessed Henry Slocum, "but fear that our losses must have been severe."

Lee continued to oversee the Confederate right. There Richard H. Anderson's division held a line between Scott's Run, just east of Catharine Furnace, and the plank road. Lafayette McLaws's brigades nestled between the plank road

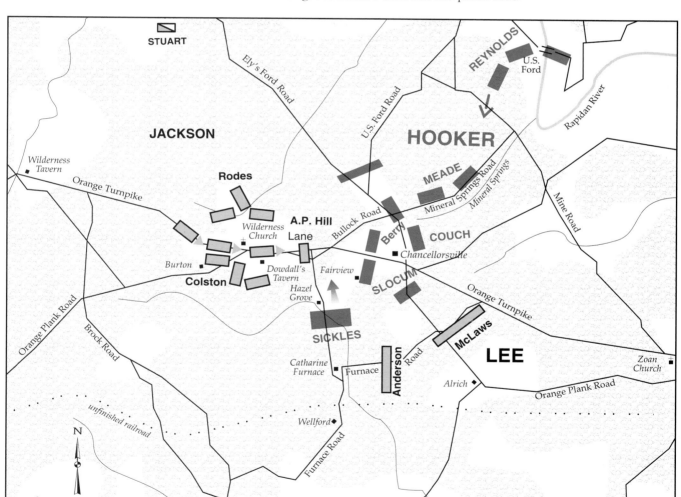

SITUATION: MAY 2, 9 P.M. – MIDNIGHT
Jackson's afternoon assault routs the Eleventh Corps, but throws Rodes's and Colston's divisions into disorder. While they reform near Wilderness Church, Jackson orders A. P. Hill's corps to the front to continue the assault. As Hill moves into position, Jackson reconnoiters in front of Lane's brigade and is injured. Sickles unsuccessfully attacks the Confederates from Hazel Grove at midnight, while Reynolds's First Corps crosses the river at U.S. Ford and hurries into position on Hooker's right.

THE WOUNDING OF JACKSON

uring a lull in the fighting, Stonewall Jackson rode out to his skirmish line on a personal reconnaissance of the Union position. As he and

members of his party were returning, a line of Confederate soldiers mistook them for Union cavalrymen and fired a volley into them. Several horsemen were hit, including Jackson, who was struck by

three bullets: two in the left arm and one in the right hand. Lieutenant Joseph G. Morrison was the general's brother-in-law and a member of his staff. In an article later published by *Confederate Veteran* magazine, he described that tragic night in the Wilderness.

"It was now nine o'clock, and Gen. Jackson, who had been for some time near the front line, rode a little in advance of it to reconnoiter the enemy's position. A heavy skirmish line had been ordered to the front, and he supposed he was in the rear of this line. He was at this time accompanied by Capt. J. K. Boswell, of the engineers, Capt. R. F. Wilburne [sic], of the signal corps, Lieut. J. G. Morrison, aid-de-camp, and five or six couriers, and had ridden but a short distance down the pike when a volley was fired at the party by the Federals in front and to the right of the road. To escape this fire the party wheeled out of the road to the left and galloped to the rear, when our own men, mistaking them for Federal cavalry making a charge, and supposing the firing in front to have been directed at the skirmish line, opened a galling fire, killing several men and horses and causing

the horses that were not struck to dash panic-stricken toward the Federal lines, which were but a very short distance in front. The General was struck in three places, and was dragged from his horse by the bough of a tree. Capt. Boswell was killed instantly.

Lieut. Morrison, leaping from his horse that was dashing into the enemy's lines, ran to an interval in our line and exclaimed: 'Cease firing! You are firing into our own men.' A colonel commanding a North Carolina regiment in Lane's Brigade cried out: 'Who gave that order? It's a lie! Pour it into them.' Morrison then ran to the colonel, told him what he had done, and assisted him to arrest the firing as soon as possible. He then went to the front in search of the General, and found him lying upon the ground, with Capt. Wilburne and Mr. Wynn, of the signal corps, bending over him examining his wounds. In a few moments Gen. Hill, accompanied by Capt. Leigh and a few couriers, rode up to where the General was lying and dismounted. On examining his wounds, they found his left arm broken near the shoulder and bleeding profusely. A handkerchief was tied around the arm, so as partially to stop

and turnpike.

Nightfall did not extinguish Stonewall Jackson's offensive spirit. He hoped renewed assaults would carry his troops to a position between the Army of the Potomac and the fords over the Rappahannock (a vain desire because thousands of Federals blocked the way and the ground favored Hooker). Jackson and a small party of riders moved east along the plank road about 9:00 P.M in search of information about the ground across which any new attacks would pass. Accompanied by a nineteen-year-old private in the Ninth

Virginia Cavalry named David Kyle, who had grown up on the Bullock farm north of Chancellorsville and thus knew local roads intimately, Jackson spurred slightly ahead of the rest of the group on the Mountain Road. That small track branched off the plank road slightly more than a mile west of Hooker's headquarters at Chancellorsville and paralleled the main route a few dozen yards to the north.

Eventually satisfied that he had ventured far enough east, Jackson turned Little Sorrel back to the west on the Mountain Road. He had covered but a short distance the bleeding.

While this was being done, and while the party were bending over the General, two Federal soldiers, with muskets cocked, stepped up to the party from behind a cluster of bushes and looked quietly on. Gen. Hill turned to several of his couriers and said in an undertone, 'Seize those men,' and it was done so quickly that they made no resistance. Lieut. Morrison, thinking these were scouts in front of an advancing line, stepped to the pike, about twenty yards distant, to see if it were so, and distinctly saw cannoneers unlimbering two pieces of artillery in the road, not a hundred yards distant.

Returning hastily, he announced this to the party, when Gen. Hill, who was now in command of the army, immediately mounted and rode to the head of Pender's column (which was coming up by the flank) to throw it into line. He left Capt. Leigh, of his staff, to assist in removing Gen. Jackson. About this time Lieutenant J. P. Smith, aide-de-camp, who had been sent to deliver an order, rode up and dismounted.

Capt. Wilburne had gone a few moments previous after a litter. The party thought it best not to await Wilburne's return, and suggested that they bear the General off in their arms, when he replied: 'No; I think I can walk.' They assisted him to rise, and supported him as he walked through the woods to the pike and toward the rear. Soon after reaching the road they obtained a litter, and placed him on it; but had not gone over forty yards when the battery in the road opened with canister. The first discharge passed over their heads; but the second was more accurate, and struck down one of the litter bearers, by which the General received a severe fall. The firing now increased in rapidity, and was so terrific that the road was soon deserted by the attendants of the General with the exception of Capt. Leigh and Lieuts. Smith and Morrison. These officers lay down in the road by the General during the firing, and could see on every side sparks flashing from the stones of the pike caused by the iron canister shot. Once the General attempted to rise, but Lieut. Smith threw his arms across his body and urged him to lie quiet a few moments, or he would certainly be killed.

After the road had been swept by this battery with a dozen or more discharges, they elevated their guns and opened with shell. So the little party now had an opportunity of removing their precious burden from the road to the woods on their right, and continued their course to the rear, carrying the General most of the way in their arms. Once they stopped that he might rest, but the fire was so heavy they thought it best to go on. The whole atmosphere seemed filled with whistling canister and shrieking shell, tearing the trees on every side. After going three or four hundred yards an ambulance was reached, containing Col. S. Crutchfield, Gen. Jackson's chief of artillery, who had just been severely wounded, a canister shot breaking his leg. The General was placed in this ambulance, and at his request one of his aids got in to support his mangled arm.

During all of this time he had scarcely uttered a groan, and expressed great sympathy for Col. Crutchfield, who was writhing under the agonies of his shattered limb. After proceeding over half a mile the ambulance reached the house of Mr. Melzi Chancellor, where a temporary hospital had been established. Here Dr. Hunter McGuire, medical director of Gen. Jackson's Corps, checked the bleeding of the General's arm and administered some stimulants. He was then taken to a field infirmary, some two miles to the rear, and about two o'clock in the night his arm was amputated by Dr. McGuire, assisted by Surgeons Black, Wells, and Coleman."

"Once the General attempted to rise, but Lieut. Smith threw his arms across his body and urged him to lie quiet a few moments, or he would certainly be killed."

when scattered shots and then a volley rang out from North Carolinians of Brigadier General James H. Lane's brigade to his left front. Struck by three balls, Jackson was helped to the ground, carried rearward, and eventually transported to a field hospital several miles behind Confederate lines where surgeons amputated his left arm. Command of the Second Corps devolved briefly on A. P. Hill, Jackson's senior lieutenant, who shortly received his own disabling wound. Authority passed finally to Jeb Stuart, summoned from his troopers during the night to take charge of the westernmost piece of the Army of Northern Virginia.

Jackson's flank attack on May 2 marked one of the most dramatic moments in Confederate military history—yet it conveyed no substantive advantage to Lee. Only Howard's corps had been seriously damaged, and the arrival at Chancellorsville of the First Corps during the night of May 2–3 more than made up for Federal losses. The two parts of Lee's army remained separated by many thousands of Hooker's soldiers. Indeed, Hooker enjoyed a situation favorable beyond the imagin-

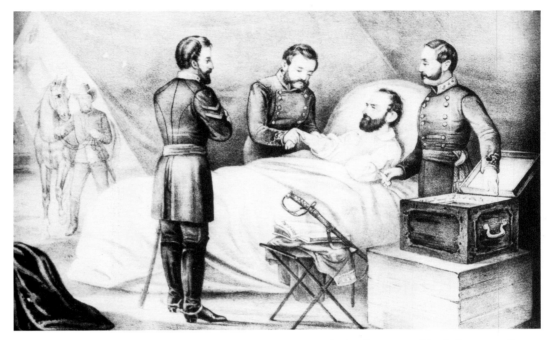

ings of most generals. With nearly 90,000 available men, he could overwhelm the much smaller forces under Stuart and Lee. Darius Couch argued vigorously after the war that the Confederate dilemma on Stuart's front was "a desperate one . . . front and right flank being in the presence of not far from 25,000 men, with the left flank subject to an assault of 30,000, [from] the corps of Meade and Reynolds." Although writing many years after the events he described, Couch still evinced passion in concluding that "it only required that Hooker should brace himself up to take a reasonable, common-sense view of the state of things, when the success gained by Jackson would have been turned into an overwhelming defeat."

But Hooker remained overawed by Lee. Thinking only of the defensive, he visited Sickles's position at Hazel Grove about dawn on Sunday, May 3. There he stood on ground that would decide the coming day's battle. The Hazel Grove plateau rose between the positions of Lee and Stuart. Almost precisely as high as Fairview and connected to that site by a clear vista through the forest, it afforded an excellent position for artillery. If Lee were to unite the divisions of Anderson and McLaws with those under Stuart—an absolute necessity for the Confederates on May 3— he must first devise a plan to wrest control of Hazel Grove from Sickles. Then Confederates could place artillery on the plateau to fire into the Twelfth Corps lines south of the plank road and west of Chancellorsville.

Hooker spared Lee the trouble of capturing Hazel Grove by ordering Sickles to abandon the position and take up a new line along the plank road. Against his better judgment (and with consequences two months hence at Gettysburg, when he saw the Peach Orchard as a comparably strong piece of ground that must be occu-pied), Sickles obediently carried out Hooker's instructions. First light had begun to penetrate the woods around the plateau when the soldiers and gunners of the Third Corps began their withdrawal. Before the last of them had departed, James J. Archer's Confederate brigade attacked from the northwest, capturing 100 prisoners and four cannon.

Archer's brigade constituted part of a broader offensive orchestrated by Jeb Stuart. The cavalryman had worked through the night to prepare Jackson's three divisions for more fighting on Sunday. As day broke with a heavy dew on the field, A. P. Hill's division (commanded by Brigadier General Henry Heth since Hill had been wounded) was nearest the Federals, Colston's in a second line 300–500 yards west, and Rodes's, which had done the hardest fighting on May 2, in a third line near Wilderness Church. All three divisions straddled the plank road. Hill's middle brigades stood just east of the works constructed earlier in the battle and then abandoned by Slocum's Federals. The divisions of Alpheus Williams and Hiram Berry faced Hill's men south and north of the road respectively.

Stuart's infantry advanced about 5:30 A.M. As soon as Archer captured Hazel

Grove, Porter Alexander, Lee's ablest artillerist, received word "to immediately crown the hill with 30 guns." "They were close at hand, and all ready," recalled Alexander, "and it was all done very quickly." The fighting west and southwest of Chancellorsville rapidly swelled into the most brutal of the campaign. The brigades of Anderson and McLaws added their weight to the attacks, pressuring the Federals from the south and southeast. Dense vegetation greeted most of the attackers. The defenders fought doggedly from behind their fieldworks. Hill's and Colston's divisions gained ground here and there, only to be driven back by Union counterattacks. Robert Rodes then threw in his brigades, which relentlessly pressed toward Fairview. On the plank road, Hiram Berry received a mortal wound. "My God, Berry, why did this have to happen?" asked a grief-stricken Joseph Hooker when he saw his lieutenant's body. "Why does the man I relied on so have to be taken away in this manner?" Not far away, Brigadier General Elisha F. Paxton of the Stonewall Brigade also lay dead. Certain he would die on May 3, Paxton had lingered over a photograph of his wife just before the battle opened. Untold others met similar fates through the early morning hours.

The élan of Stuart's infantry and superb service by Confederate artillerists helped decide the issue. Many Confederate

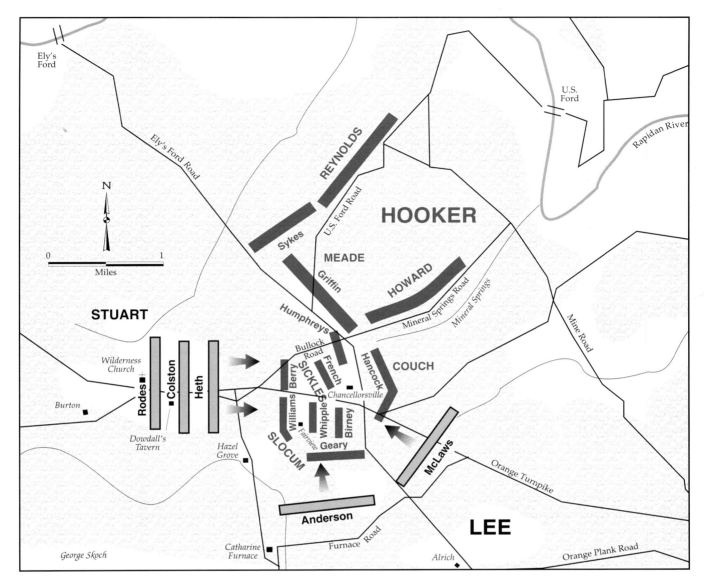

LEE ASSAILS HOOKER'S LINE: MAY 3, DAWN
At sunrise, Lee makes a determined assault against Hooker's position. Anderson and McLaws press in from the south and east, while Stuart hurls Jackson's divisions against the western face of the Union line. After four hours of heavy fighting, Hooker will abandon Chancellorsville and fall back to a new line closer to the river.

brigades seemed intent on fighting to exhaustion—none more so than Dodson Ramseur's North Carolinians, who lost upward of 750 of their 1,500 men in less than an hour. "On beholding the shattered remnants of the . . . brigade," observed an officer in one of the regiments, Ramseur "wept like a child." In support of the assaults, 20 Southern cannon along the plank road joined those at Hazel Grove to punish Union infantry and duel with 40

Federal pieces at Fairview. For the only time during the war in Virginia, Confederate gunners enjoyed a decided edge in a major engagement. Major William Ransom Johnson Pegram, just twenty-one years old and perhaps the most aggressive artillerist on the field, happily shouted to Porter Alexander amid the battle's din: "A glorious day, Colonel, a glorious day!"

Clermont Best's guns answered bravely but suffered converging fire from enemy cannon along the plank road and at Hazel Grove. Union ammunition chests ran low as Hooker ignored Best's pleas for fresh rounds. Union infantry west of Chancellorsville grudgingly gave ground on both

sides of the plank road. "My line of guns . . . kept to its work manfully until about 9 A.M.," reported Best with pride, "when, finding our infantry in front withdrawn, our right and left turned, and the enemy's musketry already so advanced as to pick off our men and horses, I was compelled to withdraw my guns to save them." The last of Best's pieces left Fairview by 9:30 A.M. A Federal counterattack briefly regained the position within half an hour, but at ten o'clock Hooker issued orders to abandon it for good. The loss of Fairview compelled abandonment of the Chancellorsville crossroads as well. Soon the Army of the Potomac was in retreat toward a defensive line nearer the Rappahannock. Parts of the Second, Third, and Twelfth corps waged a rear-guard action (Hooker had not committed their comrades in the First, Fifth, or Eleventh corps)

The soldiers of Lee and Stuart reunited shortly after ten o'clock. Forming a blazing crescent that closed in on the crossroads from the west, south, and east, Confederate infantry celebrated in wild triumph as Lee rode into the clearing around the Chancellor house. An artist could seek no more dramatic scene: Flames rose from Chancellorsville, providing a memorable

backdrop as Lee's troops shouted their devotion and exulted in their morning's accomplishment. Colonel Charles Marshall of the general's staff saw Lee astride Traveller "in the full realization of all that soldiers dream of—triumph." It must have been from such a tableau, added Marshall, "that men in ancient times rose to the dignity of gods."

The relative circumstances of Lee and Hooker at that moment graphically revealed the unequal fates of war. While Lee imbibed the adoration of his victorious soldiers, Hooker stood dazed and detached at the Bullock house a mile to the north. He had been stunned about 9:15 when a Confederate artillery projectile struck a pillar at Chancellorsville against which he was leaning. Thrown to the ground and

HOOKER APPEARED ON HORSEBACK AT THE FRONT, MAKING HIM A CONSPICUOUS TARGET FOR CONFEDERATE SHARPSHOOTERS. IN THE END, IT WAS A CANNONBALL RATHER THAN A BULLET THAT TOOK HIM OUT OF ACTION.

(NPS)

THE HEAVIEST FIGHTING OF THE CAMPAIGN TOOK PLACE ON THE MORNING OF MAY 3. IN THIS SKETCH, UNION TROOPS OF THE THIRD AND FIFTH CORPS REPEL A CONFEDERATE ASSAULT.

(NPS)

rendered briefly unconscious, Hooker had mounted unsteadily, let his troops see him, then ridden to the Bullock place, where he rested on a blanket and took some spirits. He rapidly regained a measure of lucidity, then summoned Couch to dispense instructions for withdrawing the army from Chancellorsville.

Could Lee maintain the morning's offensive momentum? His mind scarcely had time to focus on that question before alarming news arrived from Fredericksburg. John Sedgwick's men had broken

through Jubal Early's defenders and were on their way toward Chancellorsville.

Since fighting erupted in the Wilderness on the morning of May 1, Sedgwick and Early had presided over an often neglected phase of the Chancellorsville campaign. Assigned the role of occupying Lee at Fredericksburg, Sedgwick had shifted thousands of soldiers from the Sixth and First corps across the Rappahannock below town on April 29. They held their positions for three days, "assuming a threatening attitude" late on May 1 in response to orders from Hooker (orders later rescinded). Reynolds's corps departed for Chancellorsville on Saturday, May 2, leaving Sedgwick with about 24,000 men in his Sixth Corps and Brigadier General John Gibbon's division of the Second Corps. A series of orders flowed from army headquarters at Chancellorsville to Sedgwick on May 2. The last of them, dated 10:10 P.M., arrived an hour later: "The major-general commanding directs that you cross the Rappahannock at Fredericksburg on the receipt of this order, and at once take up your line of march on the Chancellorsville

THE VICTORIOUS CHIEF

On May 3, the divided wings of the Confederate army reunited in the fields surrounding the Chancellor house. Colonel Charles Marshall described the ovation accorded to Lee by the troops as he entered the clearing in his book, *An Aide-de-Camp of Lee.*

"On the morning of May 3, 1863, . . . the final assault was made upon the Federal lines at Chancellorsville. General Lee accompanied the troops in person, and as they emerged from the fierce combat they had waged in the depths of that tangled wilderness, driving the superior forces of the enemy before them across the open ground, he rode into their midst. The scene is one that can never be effaced from the minds of those who witnessed it. The troops were pressing forward with all the ardour and enthusiasm of combat. The white smoke of musketry fringed the front of the line of battle, while the artillery on the hills in the rear of the infantry shook the earth with its thunder, and filled the air with the wild shrieks of the shells that plunged into the masses of the retreating foe. To add greater horror and sublimity to the scene, Chancellor House and the woods surrounding it were wrapped in flames. In the midst of this awful scene, General Lee, mounted upon that horse which we all remember so well, rode to the front of his advancing battalions. His presence was the signal for one of those outbursts of enthusiasm which none can appreciate who have not witnessed them.

The fierce soldiers with their faces blackened with the smoke of battle, the wounded crawling with feeble limbs from the fury of the devouring flames, all seemed possessed with a common impulse. One long, unbroken cheer, in which the feeble cry of those who lay helpless on the earth blended with the strong voices of those who still fought, rose high above the roar of battle, and hailed the presence of the victorious chief. He sat in the full realization of all that soldiers dream of—triumph; and as I looked upon him in the complete fruition of the success which his genius, courage, and confidence in his army had won, I thought that it must have been from such a scene that men in ancient days rose to the dignity of gods."

CONFEDERATE ARTILLERY STRUCK THE CHANCELLOR HOUSE AND SET IT ON FIRE. FOR SEVERAL YEARS AFTER THE BATTLE, THE BUILDING LAY IN RUINS.

(USAMHI)

road until you connect with him. You will attack and destroy any force you may fall in with on the road." Although Sedgwick did not know it, Hooker expected him to retrieve Union fortunes thrown into chaos by Jackson's flank attack.

Early's instructions from Lee on May 1 had outlined a subordinate role. He was to "watch the enemy and try to hold him" at Fredericksburg, retreating toward Richmond if attacked in "overpowering numbers" or marching to Lee's support if

Sedgwick recalled all or most of his units from the Confederate side of the river. In response to garbled orders delivered by Colonel R. H. Chilton of Lee's staff on the morning of May 2, Early started most of his men toward Chancellorsville. They had progressed about a mile west on the plank road when word from William Barksdale warned that Federals had advanced in strength against a small Confederate force left at Fredericksburg. Early "determined to return at once to my former position," and

The Army of the Potomac contained thousands of new soldiers, many of whom got their first taste of combat at Chancellorsville. Among the newcomers was twenty-year-old Rice Bull of the 123rd New York Volunteers. Bull enlisted in the Union army on August 13, 1862, in response to President Lincoln's call for 300,000 additional troops, but he did not see any combat until Chancellorsville. There, he got more than his fill. On May 3, Confederate troops attacked the 123rd New York near Fairview, and in the fighting Bull fell with a bullet in his side and a shattered jaw. The following excerpt from his memoirs vividly describes the immense suffering endured by wounded soldiers, particularly those who had the misfortune of falling into enemy hands.

"I had just fired my gun and was lowering it from my shoulder when I felt a sharp sting in my face as though I had been struck with something that caused no pain. Blood began to flow down my face and neck and I knew that I had been wounded. Ransom Fisher standing next to me saw the blood streaming down my face, and said, 'You are hit. Can't I help you off?' I said, 'No, Ransom, I think I can get to the Surgeon without help.' I took my knapsack that lay on the works in front of me and started to go to the left of our Regiment where our Surgeons were located. I passed in the rear of several Companies, all were firing rapidly, and when back of Company K felt another stinging pain, this time in my left side just above the hip. Everything went black. My knapsack and gun dropped from my hands and I went down in a heap on the ground.

I do not know how long it was before I became conscious but the battle was raging furiously; two dead men who were not there when I fell were lying close to me, one across my feet. . . .

The bullet that entered my right cheek had glanced along the jaw bone and came out of my neck near the jugular vein. My second wound was in my left side above the hip; the bullet came out near the back bone making a ragged wound. It was difficult to turn either way to seek a comfortable position as I had been hit on both sides. As yet there was little pain but by night my jaw was stiff and swollen, my side was commencing to give me trouble and I was hot and feverish. The clotted blood had hardened so my clothing was chafing and irritating my wounds every time I moved. . . .

The afternoon slowly passed, a long and sorrowful one for us; then the night came, the last night on earth for many who died for the lack of the care they needed. For those not so severely wounded nature was kind, the night was beautiful, it was comfortably warm, and a full moon shone down on us, making it almost as light as day. We were so far away from the enemy's camps that we were not annoyed by them. We could faintly hear in the distance the rumble of wagons passing along the turnpike and the subdued faraway sound of fife and drum reached us. But these sounds we did not heed, for around us were suffering men and the air was filled with their cries and moans. At last it was quiet for all were so exhausted that even in the pain they slept. Before morning many died; we heard their cries no more. . . .

The morning of May 5th was bright and warm but our wounds had become so sore and we were so stiff that those of us who were able did not feel much like moving about. Many had died during the night. They were gathered up and laid side by side in the rear of a lunette that had been built by our soldiers before the battle to protect our artillery. This collection of the dead continued every day while we were in the camp and when we left scores lay there unburied. As time went on we faced a terrible condition arising from the awful odor arising from the dead horses and men that were lying all about the camp. As time went on the stench became unbearable. . . .

The morning of May 5th, Surgeons, under a flag of truce, reported at the camp. . . . They found many that required amputation; the only treatment they had for others was to give them a cerate with which to rub their wounds. The Surgeons began their bloody work at once in the immediate view of the wounded, some of whom were not more than ten feet from the table. As each amputa-

his troops "regained our former lines without trouble about ten or eleven o'clock at night." During this confusing period of march and countermarch, thought Early, Sedgwick "might have smashed every thing to pieces, but for his excessive caution."

Four Union divisions stood opposite Early's soldiers by 7:00 A.M. on May 3. John Gibbon's men were farthest north, their right resting on the Rappahannock above town. The commands of Major General John Newton, Brigadier General Albion P. Howe, and Brigadier General William T. H.

> *"The afternoon slowly passed, a long and sorrowful one for us; then the night came, the last night on earth for many who died for the lack of the care they needed."*

tion was completed the wounded man was carried to the old house and laid on the floor; the arm or leg was thrown on the ground near the table, only a few feet from the wounded who were laying near by. . . .

About noon thunder heads began to form in the west and south and before one in the afternoon we heard the sound of thunder. . . . It was about two in the afternoon when the storm started; it lasted about two hours. . . .

The condition of most of the wounded was deplorable. More than half had no tent covering, so had to take the full force of the storm. Many could not move without help; they lay in the gutters between the rows, and were half submerged. A few had the strength to sit up in the muddy pool but the greater part lay sprawled in the mud and filth with nothing between them and the ground but their soaked woolen blankets. Many did not even have a blanket. I saw many men lying in from three to five inches of water. We were told, though I did not see this, that on the east side of the cabin two men were drowned. They were lying close under the eaves and were unable to move when they were covered by the water that fell from the roof. . . .

The night came and the rain increased. Those who were fortunate enough to have a tent sat up, back to back to brace each other, either shivering with chills or burning with fever from their wounds. There were no lights about the camp, the darkness was impenetrable, and the groans and shrieks of the wounded could be heard on

every side. . . . Not a thing had been done officially [by the Confederate army] either for or against us who lay wounded. We were entirely ignored and were to all appearance of no more consequence than the dead horses that lay around us.

Starvation that had threatened for several days became acute. The badly wounded were getting weaker every hour and even the stronger were breaking down. Wounds were feverish and festering and hunger was now adding to our troubles; food was as necessary as nursing. Great numbers were still laying in the mud, helpless. There were no privy vaults, but had there been the majority were too weak to go to them. There still remained nearly five hundred men in the camp. I must leave it to your imagination for I cannot describe these awful conditions, which were made worse by the stench from the dead men and horses. None of the men or horses had been buried. The horses lay where they had died, the men lay in a row side by side south of the cabin in sight of all the wounded. . . .

By May 8th our wounds had all festered and were hot with fever; our clothing which came in contact with them was so filthy and stiff from the dried blood that it gravely aggravated our condition. Many wounds developed gangrene and blood poisoning; lockjaw caused suf-

fering and death. While the stench from nearby dead horses and men was sickening it was not worse than that from the living who lay in their own filth. Finally, not the least of our troubles were the millions of flies that filled the air and covered blood-saturated clothing when they could not reach and sting the unbandaged wounds. As days went by none of these conditions improved, except the cries of the mortally wounded gradually lessened as they, one by one, were carried away and laid by the side of those who had gone before them."

Bull remained on the battlefield for nine days, until May 12, when Union ambulances arrived under a flag of truce and carried him back to safety across the Rappahannock River. He survived his wounds and returned to his regiment within a year. He died in 1930 at the age of eighty-eight.

— Excerpts from Rice Bull's memoirs courtesy of Presidio Press, Novato, CA.

CRUDE FARM BUILDINGS, LIKE THOSE PICTURED HERE, FREQUENTLY SERVED AS FIELD HOSPITALS DURING THE BATTLES. IN MANY INSTANCES, WOUNDED SOLDIERS HAD NO SHELTER AT ALL.

(NPS)

Brooks—all Sixth Corps divisions—ran from Fredericksburg south across Deep Run. Early's line defended everything from the plank road to a point well beyond Brooks's position. Barksdale's Mississippians held the Confederate left; Early understandably allocated most of his men to the right, where

Burnside's Federals had achieved their only success in the battle of Fredericksburg five months earlier. A last-minute adjustment shifted Brigadier General Harry T. Hays's Louisiana brigade from the far right to Barksdale's left. A thin line of men from the Twenty-first and Eighteenth Mississippi, sup-

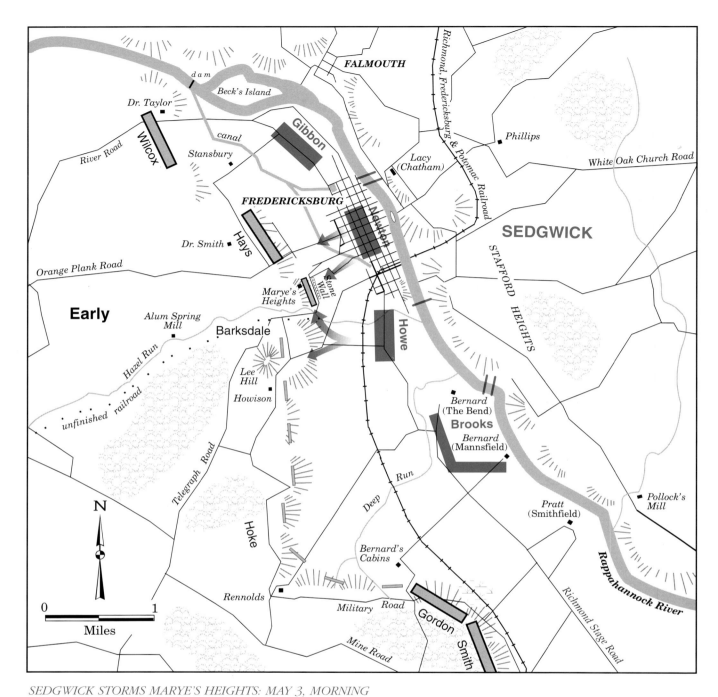

SEDGWICK STORMS MARYE'S HEIGHTS: MAY 3, MORNING
Early holds a seven-mile-long line on the hills behind Fredericksburg with a force of roughly 9,000 men. At dawn, Sedgwick marches into town from the south, clearing the way for Gibbon's division to cross, and at 10 A.M. carries the heights with a head-on assault. Early retreats south along the Telegraph Road, while Sedgwick regroups his corps and heads west toward Chancellorsville.

ported by the Washington Artillery of New Orleans, watched alertly from behind the famous stone wall that bordered the sunken road below the crest of Marye's Heights.

Union attackers probed the Confederate lines at mid-morning. Twice they recoiled from the stone wall, leaving many casualties—among them nearly a third of the Fifth Wisconsin and the Sixth Maine and almost 40 percent of the Seventh Massachusetts—scattered on the infamous killing ground of December 1862. Searing memories of that earlier slaughter doubtless troubled many a Union observer. After the second repulse, Colonel Thomas M. Griffin of the Eighteenth Mississippi unwisely allowed a few Federals to approach the stone wall under a flag of truce. Ostensibly collecting wounded comrades, these men discovered how few defenders manned this part of Early's line. Soon a third wave of attackers ascended the heights. "When the signal forward is given," Colonel Thomas S. Allen shouted to his Fifth Wisconsin, "you will start at double-quick, you will not fire a gun, and you will not stop until you get the order to halt. You will never get that order!" Within minutes Federals surged over the Confederate line, capturing scores of prisoners and eight cannon.

Jubal Early kept his head and conducted a skillful retreat along the Telegraph Road, putting together a defensive line near the Cox house some two and a half miles south of Marye's Heights. A gunner who had escaped capture on the heights spoke for other Confederates involved in the morning's debacle: "I reckon now the people of the Southern Confederacy," he said sarcastically, "are satisfied that Barksdale's brigade and the Washington Artillery can't whip the whole damned Yankee army!"

An open plank road beckoned John Sedgwick westward toward

Chancellorsville. But the Sixth Corps chief, whose reputation then and now has been much inflated, frittered away precious time forming a column of march. When the Federals finally got moving, with Brooks's division in the lead followed by Newton's and Howe's, they ran into a pesky brigade of five Alabama regiments commanded by Brigadier General Cadmus Marcellus Wilcox. Deployed early that morning at

UNION TROOPS OVERWHELMED BARKSDALE'S MISSISSIPPIANS IN THE SUNKEN ROAD, THEN SWARMED UP MARYE'S HEIGHTS CAPTURING EIGHT GUNS, INCLUDING SIX FROM THE FAMOUS WASHINGTON ARTILLERY.

(BL)

Banks Ford on the Rappahannock, Wilcox had marched his troops toward Fredericksburg in time to witness the loss of Marye's Heights. "I felt confident, if forced to retire along the Plank Road," he wrote in his report of the day's action, "that I could do so without precipitancy, and that ample time could be given for re-enforcements to reach us from Chancellorsville." Wilcox spent the next several hours executing a textbook delaying action. He disputed Sedgwick's progress first on a ridge about 800 yards west of Marye's Heights, again north of the Downman house, a third time at the toll gate on the plank road not quite three and a half miles west of Fredericksburg, and finally along a ridge at Salem Church, a modest brick Baptist meetinghouse standing 1,000 yards beyond the toll gate on the south side of the road.

Just as Wilcox predicted, reinforcements from Chancellorsville joined him at Salem Church. Lafayette McLaws brought three of his brigades and one of

Anderson's, boosting Confederate strength to nearly 10,000 men. The Rebel line extended a mile and a quarter, drawn south to north across the plank road and facing east. Wilcox's brigade occupied the center, with two regiments north and three south of the road. The brigades of Brigadier General Paul J. Semmes and William Mahone extended Wilcox's right, those of Brigadier General Joseph B. Kershaw and Brigadier General William T. Wofford his left.

The battle of Salem Church opened late in the afternoon when Union artillery near the toll gate exchanged fire with southern guns. About 5:30, two brigades of Brooks's division launched a determined assault along both sides of the plank road. Brigadier General Joseph J. Bartlett's mixed command of New York, Pennsylvania, and Maine regiments advanced south of the road. Colonel Emory Upton's 121st New York penetrated to the church grounds before being driven back toward the toll gate. The brigade lost 580 of its 1,500 men:

CADMUS WILCOX

(BL)

"It was the first time they were ever repulsed . . .," affirmed a proud Bartlett, "and their losses attest their regret more feelingly than I can express it." Across the road, Colonel Henry W. Brown's New Jersey brigade, supported by part of Newton's division, failed to breach the Rebel line. Nightfall terminated what Sedgwick called a "sharp and prolonged contest." Wilcox characterized the Federal effort as "a bloody repulse to the enemy, rendering entirely useless to him his little success of the morning at Fredericksburg."

Both armies remained divided on the night of May 3–4. Although unwilling to act offensively himself against Lee's vastly outnumbered force at Chancellorsville, Hooker criticized Sedgwick for moving lethargically. "My object in ordering General Sedgwick forward . . . was to relieve me from the position in which I found myself at Chancellorsville . . . ," asserted Hooker shortly after the battle. "In my judgment General Sedgwick did not

obey the spirit of my order, and made no sufficient effort to obey it. . . . When he did move, it was not with sufficient confidence or ability on his part to manoeuvre his troops." A Confederate critic of the operations agreed that Sedgwick had "wasted great opportunities, & come about as near to doing nothing with 30,000 men as it was easily possible to do." In truth, neither Hooker nor Sedgwick displayed leadership on May 3 worthy of the soldiers who fought under their charge. Moreover, Hooker's expectation that one-fifth of his army should rescue the other four-fifths demonstrated the degree to which he quaked before the specter of R. E. Lee.

Lee typically had labored throughout May 3 to find some way to punish the Federals. He divided his army yet a third time by dispatching McLaws to reinforce Wilcox. Hooker's six corps hunkered behind a great U-shaped complex of earthworks with both flanks anchored on the Rappahannock, protecting United States Ford. Because the Federal commander dis-

JOHN SEDGWICK BROKE THROUGH JUBAL EARLY'S THIN LINE AT FREDERICKSBURG, ONLY TO BE STOPPED AT SALEM CHURCH. HOOKER LATER CRITICIZED HIM FOR MOVING TOO SLOWLY.

(NA)

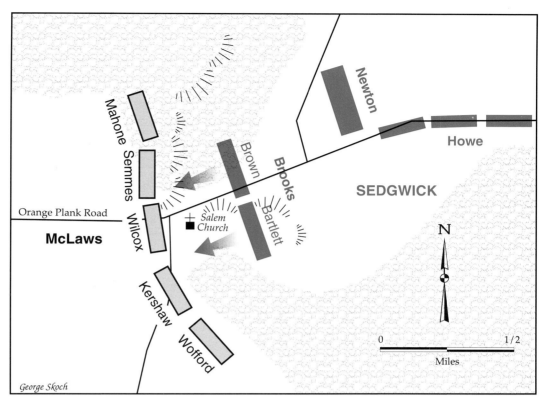

George Skoch

THE BATTLE OF SALEM CHURCH: MAY 3, 5:30 P.M.
After carrying Marye's Heights in the morning, Sedgwick pushes west toward
Chancellorsville. Wilcox's brigade delays Sedgwick's march, then falls back to Salem
Church, where it is joined by four additional brigades led by McLaws. Sedgwick attacks the
Confederate line late in the afternoon, but is unable to break through.

played no hint of aggressiveness, Lee believed four divisions to be sufficient strength at Chancellorsville. Jeb Stuart

eventually spread Hill's, Colston's, and Rodes's commands across a two-mile front south of Hooker's works; three brigades of Richard Anderson's division blocked the Old Mine Road where it crossed the River Road, thereby denying Hooker a direct route between the wings of his army. When sounds of fighting at Salem Church drifted westward to Lee's position, the Confederate commander sent messages urging Early and McLaws to cooperate in a joint attack against Sedgwick.

These messages arrived after dark—too late for action on May 3—but Early immediately informed McLaws that he would gather his brigades during the night for an attack on May 4. Sedgwick's corps held a strong position, its flanks on

the Rappahannock covering Banks' Ford and its center bulging across the plank road. From south and southeast of Sedgwick, Early's troops would attempt to drive the enemy off Marye's Heights and other high ground west of Fredericksburg, cut Sedgwick off from the town, and pressure the eastern flank of the Sixth Corps. McLaws's five brigades lay west and southwest of Sedgwick. During the advance, Early would extend his left to touch McLaws's right brigade, thus achieving Lee's goal of a combined assault. The army commander sent a message to McLaws dated midnight on May 3 approving Early's plan "if it is practicable" and

THIS POSTWAR VIEW
OF THE ORANGE PLANK
ROAD LOOKS EAST
FROM SALEM CHURCH.
ON MAY 3, SEDGWICK'S
TROOPS FORMED IN THE
LOW GROUND VISIBLE IN
THE DISTANCE AND
ATTACKED ASTRIDE
THE ROAD TOWARD
THE VIEWER.

(NPS)

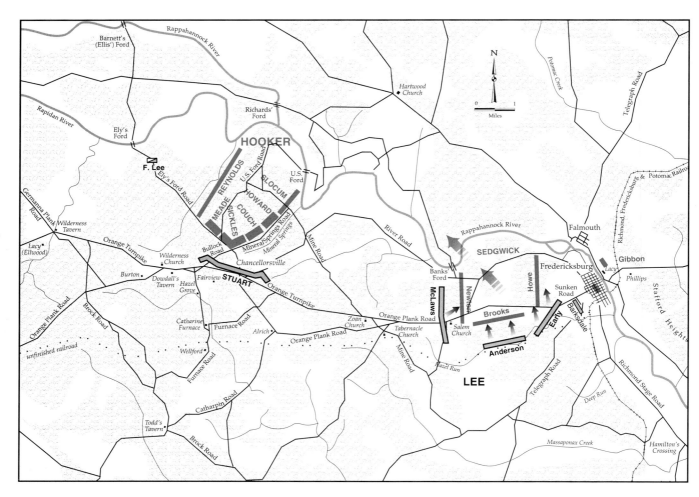

SEDGWICK RETREATS: MAY 4
Lee leads Anderson's division to Salem Church and joins forces there with McLaws and Early in attacking Sedgwick. Sedgwick successfully resists the Confederates until dark, then retreats across Banks' Ford. Finding himself cut off from Sedgwick by the Confederates, Gibbon too retreats. Stuart meanwhile keeps an eye on Hooker, who holds a strong entrenched position covering U.S. Ford.

requesting that McLaws engage the Federals "so as to prevent their concentrating on General Early."

A promising Confederate start on May 4 soon gave way to frustration. Early's brigades easily reoccupied Marye's and adjacent heights, but the stolid McLaws refused to budge. Lee arrived at Salem Church with the balance of Anderson's division before noon. Approximately 21,000 Confederates now slightly outnumbered Sedgwick's Federals. Even Lee's presence failed to galvanize his two senior subordinates, however, and several hours slipped away as Anderson maneuvered his

troops into position and McLaws remained a contented bystander. Jubal Early fumed at the loss of precious time. The delays also left Lee angry—thwarted in his desire to hurl every available Confederate soldier against Sedgwick.

Time hung equally heavy along the Union lines. Hooker communicated virtually nothing helpful to Sedgwick, who thought mainly of how to protect his line of retreat to Banks' Ford. A Union colonel recalled the day's building tension: "All the afternoon we watched the Rebels moving through the woods on our front, and every now and then uttering the Rebel yell, at

LAFAYETTE MCLAWS STOPPED SEDGWICK AT SALEM CHURCH ON MAY 3, BUT HIS HESITATION THE NEXT DAY ALLOWED HIS ADVERSARY TO ESCAPE.

(BL)

times apparently forming into lines of battle and preparing to attack. It was one of the most anxious six or seven hours that I ever spent." A staff officer expressed the hope to Sedgwick that "if the Sixth Corps goes out of existence today . . . it will be with a blaze of glory." "I will tell you a secret," replied the general with a grim smile, "there will be no surrendering."

The Confederates finally attacked shortly before 6:00 P.M. Two of Early's

brigades—Harry Hays's Louisianians and Brigadier General Robert F. Hoke's North Carolinians—advanced vigorously and gained a foothold across the plank road on Sedgwick's left center. Anderson's division showed considerably less spirit, and McLaws's soldiers contributed nothing to the assault. After the war, Fitzhugh Lee expressed bafflement at McLaws's behavior. "I know the difference between hindsight & foresight," he stated in a letter to Jubal Early, "but between you & I, what was the matter with McLaws in connection with the attack on Sedgwick on Tuesday 4th May!"

Just as Lee had heard the firing at Salem Church on the afternoon of May 3, so also did Hooker hear it on Monday. Snug behind his bristling lines, he took no steps to assist Sedgwick. In his postwar recollections, Southern artillerist Porter Alexander evinced contempt for Hooker's lack of action on May 4: "I've sometimes thought that if we had given Sedgwick a big fight that morning the noise of the guns & musketry must have stirred Hooker for very shame to put his big force in motion at Chancellorsville."

The curiously bungled Confederate offensive at Salem Church on May 4 marked the end of significant fighting during the Chancellorsville campaign.

The curiously bungled Confederate offensive at Salem Church on May 4 marked the end of significant fighting during the Chancellorsville campaign.

AFTER ABANDONING CHANCELLORSVILLE, HOOKER TOOK UP A STRONG DEFENSIVE LINE COVERING U.S. FORD. UNION SOLDIERS INCORPORATED LOGS, KNAPSACKS, LIMBER CHESTS, AND EVEN DEAD HORSES INTO THE WORKS—WHATEVER HAPPENED TO BE AT HAND.

(BL)

A Union Surgeon at Salem Church

Among those captured on May 4, 1863, in the Union retreat to Scott's Ford was Dr. Daniel Holt, a surgeon in the 121st New York Volunteers. After being confined overnight in a house on the battlefield, Holt received permission to care for the wounded Union soldiers housed inside of Salem Church. The following excerpt, taken from a letter written by Holt on May 15, 1863, less than two weeks after the battle, describes his labors at the church and the assistance he received from Confederate officers.

"Worn out by fatigue and faint through want of proper food (for I had for the three days previous, neither seen meat or bread, and had slept but a very few hours during all that time) I went to work, more dead than alive, but with a will which in some degree compensated, and thus struggled on for four days longer until help arrived from our side of the river. When I now look back upon those days so full of incidents and suffering, I can hardly realize that I have passed through it, and am still alive. Yet I worked and staggered on until it seemed as if I could not drag one foot before another; and while bending over the bodies of our boys dressing their wounds, my eyes, in spite of me, would close, and I have found myself fast asleep over a dying man. Had not General Wilcox (Confederate) kindly supplied me with food from his own table, and made me a guest rather than a prisoner, I believe I should have been compelled to throw myself down with the rest and crave the treatment I myself was yielding. As it was, I kept about, being the recipient of numerous favors from rebel officers, always treated with respect, and in very many cases with marked kindness. Here General Lee came to see me. Four times did this great man call and feelingly inquire if the men were receiving all the care that could be bestowed: at the same time remarking that it was beyond his power to yield such succor as his heart prompted. Their army, he remarked, was not supplied as ours, with Sanitary and Christian Commission supplies, neither was the Medical department as completely and thoroughly equipped—no chloroform for minor cases of Surgery—no stimulents for moderate or severe prostration, and as a consequence no means of alleviating the suffering of their men,—

All that he could do, he did do: he sent the Medical Director of their army to look in upon us and to supply help in amputations &c., which by this time had become imperative. Death was upon our track and most nobly did these Surgeons combat it. Not alone in the breasts of our men dwell humanity. Human nature is about the same the world over, and I found just as sympathetic hearts here as anywhere. I must in justice say for an enemy, that I never was treated with greater consideration by intelligent men, than I was by these very rebs for the ten days I remained among them; and at the same time I might say I never had so hard a time. The experience of a life time was crowded into these eventful days."

— Excerpt from
A Surgeon's Civil War: The Letters and Diary of Daniel M. Holt, M.D., courtesy of Kent State University Press.

AFTER THE BATTLE, UNION AND CONFEDERATE SURGEONS CONVERTED SALEM CHURCH INTO A FIELD HOSPITAL. "THE AMPUTATED LIMBS WERE PILED UP IN EVERY CORNER ALMOST AS HIGH AS A MAN COULD REACH," ONE GEORGIA COLONEL RECALLED, "BLOOD FLOWED IN STREAMS ALONG THE AISLES AND OUT AT THE DOORS."

(NPS)

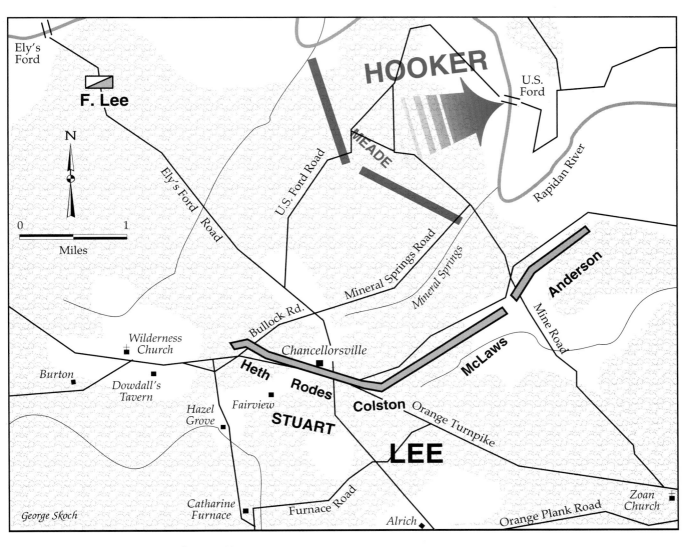

HOOKER RETREATS: MAY 5–6, NIGHT

Having eliminated the threat to his rear, Lee returns to Chancellorsville to finish off Hooker, but the Union commander declines to give battle. Learning of Sedgwick's retreat and anticipating an attack on his own line, Hooker instead orders the army to withdraw across U.S. Ford. Meade's corps covers the retreat.

Sedgwick withdrew across Banks' Ford early the next morning, freeing Lee to hurry back to Chancellorsville for one last effort against Hooker. Although still badly outnumbered, the Confederate commander issued orders for his artillery to select positions from which to enfilade Hooker's powerful line. The projected attacks, which almost certainly would have been bloody failures, never materialized because during the night of May 4–5 Hooker decided to retreat. He first went through the charade of requesting counsel from his corps commanders. Five weary major generals met at army headquarters at midnight (Slocum

and Sedgwick were absent). Reynolds, Meade, and Howard voted to attack Lee. Couch and Sickles preferred to retreat. After the men had voiced their opinions, Hooker announced his intention to recross the Rappahannock. "What was the use of calling us together at this time of night," Reynolds grumbled to Couch as they left Hooker's tent, "when he intended to retreat anyhow?"

Driving rain soaked Union soldiers tramping toward the pontoon bridges at United States Ford on May 5. Many grew despondent when they realized Hooker meant to abandon the field. A soldier in

50

the 141st Pennsylvania voiced a common sentiment: "We supposed that our men still held the heights of Fredericksburg—that although we were lying comparatively quiet our men were doing a big thing elsewhere," he commented. "And then the thought, must we lose this battle? Have these brave comrades who have fought so bravely and died at their post died in vain?" Confederates such as cartographer Jedediah Hotchkiss marveled that Hooker had given up so easily. After a day of taking measurements in the area for a map of the campaign, Hotchkiss recorded in his journal on May 12, 1863, that he "had no idea the enemy were so well fortified and wonder they left their works so soon." Such speculation lay ahead as unit after unit of the Army of the Potomac trudged

across their pontoons on May 5-6. By 9:00 A.M. on Wednesday the sixth, the last Federals had reached the left bank of the Rappahannock. Union engineers pulled the soggy pontoon bridges from the Rappahannock, bringing to an end the latest—and in many ways the most promising—Union operation against Lee and the Army of Northern Virginia.

News of Chancellorsville reverberated through the North and the Confederacy. When Abraham Lincoln learned of the retreat, he began to pace nervously, moaning, "My God! My God! What will the country say? What will the country say?" Editor Horace Greeley of the *New York Tribune* reacted almost identically: "My God!" he said, holding the telegram that announced the chilling news, "it is horrible—horrible; and to think of it, 130,000 magnificent soldiers so cut to pieces by less than 60,000 half-starved ragamuffins!" On the home front and within the Army of the Potomac, various villains were put forward—O. O. Howard and his Germans for being routed on May 2, John Sedgwick for failing to march with alacrity on the third or to fight harder on the fourth, and of course Joseph Hooker, whose blustering before the campaign had set him up for a spectacular fall. Whispers suggested that the commanding general had been drunk, a charge difficult to substantiate or deny from surviving evidence.

Hooker sought to justify his own performance. A congratulatory order to the army betrayed only the remotest connection to reality. "In withdrawing from the south bank of the Rappahannock before delivering a general battle to our adversaries," it read in part, "the army has given renewed evidence of its confidence in itself and its fidelity to the principles it represents." Hooker spoke with a group of officers in late May, defending his decision to remain passive on May 4 with the observation that he expected Lee to assault the Union works. He also expressed anger toward Sedgwick at this gathering. "He was very bitter against 'Uncle John,'" wrote a colonel from the First Corps who heard the comments, "accusing him of being slow and afraid to fight; also of disobeying orders directly." Offended by Hooker's statements, this officer felt "shame for my commanding general, and indignation at the attack on so true, brave, and modest a man as Sedgwick." Some officers in the Army of the Potomac saw justice in Hooker's travails after Chancellorsville, pleased that the man who had pilloried Burnside after Fredericksburg now gagged on a dose of his own medicine.

Most reaction south of the Mason-Dixon Line mirrored that of Catharine Ann Devereux Edmondston, a North Carolina woman who described relatives on May 10 "full of our Victory, which all admit to be a glorious one, throwing that of Fredericksburg in the shade." As did many other happy Confederates, she alluded to numbers and the fact that Chancellorsville represented but the latest in a series of Lee's triumphs: "Hooker is terribly beaten & that too by a force one half his own. Off with his head & let him too take a house in N Y & join the clique of beaten Generals—'Beaten Row' or 'Vanquished Square' or 'Conquered Place' and call it as their taste may be." Jefferson Davis thanked Lee and his army "in the name of the people . . . for this addition to the unprecedented series of great victories which your army has achieved." Lee's vet-

When Abraham Lincoln learned of the retreat, he began to pace nervously, moaning, "My God! My God! What will the country say?"

A CURRIER AND IVES LITHOGRAPH OF THE BATTLE OF CHANCELLORSVILLE, MAY 3, 1863.

(LC)

erans joined many civilian counterparts in redoubling their faith in a commander seemingly able to accomplish the impossible. If the Army of Northern Virginia could vanquish Hooker's "finest army on the planet" with Longstreet and two full divisions absent, what could prevent its carry-

STONEWALL JACKSON'S LAST DAY

After being wounded at Chancellorsville, Stonewall Jackson was carried behind the lines to the Wilderness Tavern, where Doctor Hunter H. McGuire removed his injured left arm just two inches below the shoulder. The general was then taken by horse-drawn ambulance a distance of 27 miles to Guinea Station on the R. F. & P. Railroad, where he would rest before continuing on to Richmond. For six days he remained at Guinea, occupying the farm office of Thomas Chandler's home,

"Fairfield." At first, he showed signs of recovery, but later in the week pneumonia set in and by Sunday, May 10, doctors gave up all hope of his recovery. In the following account, Dr. McGuire recalled the general's quiet faith and courage in the final hours of his life.

"About daylight, on Sunday morning, Mrs. Jackson informed him that his recovery was very doubtful, and that it was better that he should be prepared for the worst. He was silent for a moment, and then

said: 'It will be infinite gain to be translated to Heaven.' He advised his wife, in the event of his death, to return to her father's house, and added, 'You have a kind and good father, but there is no one so kind and good as your Heavenly Father.' He still expressed a hope of his recovery, but requested her, if he should die, to have him buried in Lexington, in the Valley of Virginia. His exhaustion increased so rapidly, that at eleven o'clock, Mrs. Jackson knelt by his bed, and told him that before the sun went down,

AFTER THE AMPUTATION OF HIS LEFT ARM, JACKSON WAS CARRIED 27 MILES TO GUINEA STATION. HE SPENT THE LAST WEEK OF HIS LIFE AT FAIRFIELD, THE HOME OF THOMAS CHANDLER.

(NPS)

ing the nascent Southern nation toward independence?

Lee took a far more subdued view. "At Chancellorsville we gained another victory; our people were wild with delight—" he stated shortly after Gettysburg. "I, on the contrary, was more depressed than after Fredericksburg; our loss was severe, and again we had gained not an inch of ground and the enemy could not be pursued." Indeed, Chancellorsville was a bittersweet success. Lee lost nearly 13,000 men killed, wounded, and missing— 22 percent of his entire army. In contrast, the Union butcher's bill was relatively

much lower, slightly more than 17,000 casualties that amounted to 13 percent of Hooker's force. Worst of all for Lee and the Confederacy, Stonewall Jackson died on May 10 of complications arising from injuries he received while being carried from the field on May 2. Lee would never find an adequate replacement for the strange and compelling genius he called the "great and good" Jackson.

Although he viewed Chancellorsville as an empty victory, Lee took away from it even deeper admiration for his soldiers. "With heartfelt gratification," he announced in General Orders No. 59 on May 7, 1863, he would be with his Saviour. He replied, 'Oh, no! you are frightened, my child; death is not so near; I may yet get well.' She fell over upon the bed, weeping bitterly, and told him again that the physicians said there was no hope. After a moment's pause he asked her to call me. 'Doctor, Anna informs me that you have told her that I am to die to-day; it is so?' When he was answered, he turned his eyes towards the ceiling, and gazed for a moment or two, as if in intense thought, then replied, 'Very good, very good, it is all right.' He then tried to comfort his almost heart-broken wife, and told her he had a good deal to say to her, but he was too weak. Colonel Pendleton came into the room about one o'clock, and he asked him, 'Who was preaching at head-quarters to-day?' When told that the whole army was praying for him, he replied, 'Thank God—they are very kind.' He said: 'It is the Lord's Day; my wish is fulfilled. I have always desired to die on Sunday.'

His mind now began to fail and wander, and he frequently talked as if in command upon the field, giving orders in his old way; then the scene shifted, and he was at the mess-table, in conversation

with members of his staff; now with his wife and child; now at prayers with his military family. Occasional intervals of return of his mind would appear, and during one of them, I offered him some brandy and water, but he declined it, saying, 'It will only delay my departure, and do no good; I want to preserve my mind, if possible, to the last.' About half-past one, he was told that he had but two hours to live, and he answered again, feebly, but firmly, 'Very good, it is all right.' A few moments before

he died he cried out in his delirium, 'Order A. P. Hill to prepare for action! pass the infantry to the front rapidly! tell Major Hawks'—then stopped, leaving the sentence unfinished. Presently, a smile of ineffable sweetness spread itself over his pale face, and he said quietly, and with an expression, as if of relief, 'Let us cross over the river, and rest under the shade of the trees;' and then, without pain, or the least struggle, his spirit passed from earth to the God who gave it."

ON MAY 10, JACKSON BREATHED HIS LAST. HIS FINAL WORDS WERE, "LET US CROSS OVER THE RIVER, AND REST UNDER THE SHADE OF THE TREES."

(NPS)

CANNONS AT HAZEL GROVE.

(NPS)

military leadership can accomplish against daunting obstacles. Would a better Union general have made Lee pay dearly for the risks he took? Perhaps so—but it was Joseph Hooker who faced the Confederate paladin in the Wilderness of Spotsylvania, and his personality looms as large in any modern consideration of the campaign as it did in Lee's calculations at the time. The men of the Army of the Potomac, who had fought so well on so many fields only to be betrayed by their commanders, once again showed robust devotion to duty at Chancellorsville. But the lion's share of accolades must go to Lee and the Army of Northern Virginia, whose daring and perseverance concocted a tactical victory of memorable proportion. Chancellorsville capped a string of triumphs for Lee's army in Virginia that nurtured among the Confederate citizenry an expectation of continued success. That expectation in turn would sustain hopes for Southern independence during two more years of grinding war.

"the general commanding expresses to the army his sense of the heroic conduct displayed by officers and men during the arduous operations in which they have just been engaged." The result, asserted Lee, entitled the army "to the praise and gratitude of the nation." Perhaps Chancellorsville convinced Lee that his men could overcome any odds. Whether or not that was the case, his profound belief in their skill and devotion manifested itself two months later in crucial decisions at Gettysburg.

Although it was the bloodiest battle to that stage of the Civil War, Chancellorsville rapidly receded from the front pages as Lee marched north in June. The eastern armies soon reached their fateful rendezvous at Gettysburg, where unprecedented carnage pushed the events of early May well into the shadows. Yet Chancellorsville retains a timeless fascination as an example of what imaginative